LEGENDARY WAR MOVIES

LEGENDARY WAR MOVIES

Peter Guttmacher

MetroBooks

An Imprint of Friedman/Fairfax Publishers

© 1996 by Michael Friedman Publishing Group, Inc.

Library of Congress Cataloging-in-Publication data available upon request.

ISBN 1-56799-240-4

Editor: Benjamin Boyington
Art Director: Lynne Yeamans
Designer: Jan Melchior
Photography Editor: Kathryn Culley
Photography Researcher: Darrell Perry

Color separations by Ocean Graphic International Company Ltd.
Printed in China by Leefung-Asco Printers Ltd.

For bulk purchases and special sales, please contact:
Friedman / Fairfax Publishers
Attention: Sales Department
15 West 26th Street
New York, NY 10010
212/685-6610 FAX 212/685-1307

Visit the Friedman/Fairfax Website:
http://www.webcom.com/friedman

ACKNOWLEDGMENTS

The author would like to salute the guidance and tactical support of Admiral Ben Boyington and Chief Recruiting Officer Elizabeth Sullivan, as well as the invaluable assistance of the entire Fleet Staff at the Academy of Motion Picture Arts and Sciences' Margaret Herrick Research Library. He also wishes to acknowledge the advisement of Field Marshals Richard Guttmacher and Paul Davenport, as well as the dedication of Captain Mark Schwind and the rest of the front line troops at Rocket Video. Most of all, he extends his gratitude to Rear Gunner Robin Brownstein for her marksmanship during the final stages of the campaign, and for sitting through so much bloodshed.

DEDICATION

This book of war is dedicated in peace and love to the memory of Ann E. Guttmacher.

CONTENTS

Warriors come in all shapes, colors, and sizes. You don't want to mess with this sixteenth-century warlord, especially if you're his father in master filmmaker Akira Kurosawa's tribute to Shakespeare's King Lear *and Japanese legend—the spectacular* Ran *(1985).*

INTRODUCTION

War. No act of mankind is larger in scope. No other event is as impersonal and meticulous in its planning, as personal and chaotic in its execution, and as international in its effect. No undertaking is as horrendously expensive, potentially profitable, or emotionally volatile. It almost sounds like a description of moviemaking, doesn't it?

War movies. Those worth remembering are driven not merely by battles and not just by bloodshed, but by our biggest fears and passions. With all its drama, its tests of human nature, and its focus on technology, what could be better fare for film than warfare? But the long lines of moviegoers waiting to see such blockbusters as *Platoon* and *Schindler's List* didn't just come from around the block.

They have woven their way through a far-reaching, fascinating, and often fickle evolution in popular moviegoing and American war consciousness. Patriotism, loss, heroism, violence, family, strategy, adventure, compassion, and rebellion—these concepts are deeply rooted in any nation. To find the very first person standing on line for a popular war picture, we would have to turn back the clock at least eighty years.

In 1914, the American motion picture industry was almost twenty years old—certainly of draft age. The tiny, two-minute-long filmettes with which France's appropriately named Lumière brothers had first illuminated Paris and the similarly slim, slice-of-life vignettes that the legendary Thomas Alva Edison had put on the screen only four months later in New York had grown by leaps and bounds. So had the filmgoing public's interest in films about armed combat.

The first "cinematic vignettes" included clips of quick-draw cartoonist Tom Merry and his 1895 renderings of Germany's Kaiser Wilhelm and Prussia's Count Bismarck. By 1899, film had found its way to the front lines as British production companies sent cameramen to South Africa to shoot the Boer War. Soon, newsreels like *A Skirmish with the Boers Near Kimberly by a Troop of Cavalry Scouts Attached to General French's Column* were drawing Britishers to the cinema. But these films weren't exactly captivating; the flat, often distant scenes of warfare they featured lacked dramatic interest. Directors remedied that situation by lacing the real combat footage with carefully staged (and often bloodier) scenes shot in Blackburn, Lancashire—not darkest Africa.

Patriotic as well as picaresque, turn-of-the-century newsreels covered military conflicts of all kinds. In 1900, to honor the Boxer Rebellion in China, filmmaker James Williamson and his family used his own English garden to simulate the *Attack on a Chinese Mission* (burning down a cottage in the process). Other films creatively dealt with America's 1901 involvement in the Philippines, the Russo-Japanese War of 1904, and the 1907 unrest in Belfast and Morocco.

The "effect" wasn't lost on the audiences or filmmakers of the United States. Edison's production company followed in British footsteps, creating dramatically doctored newsreels of many of the same conflicts. Nor was the propaganda power of the films overlooked. The Spanish-American War of 1898 was fomented, chronicled, and sold to the public by other media besides William Randolph Hearst's newspaper headlines.

Films like *Tearing Down the Spanish Flag* (1897), which was, in fact, shot on a stateside rooftop, had an effect on public opinion. Filmmaker Edward H. Amet staged the sinking of Admiral Cervera's fleet at Santiago in his bathtub by blasting model ships. He later claimed that the footage had been shot with a telescopic lens from a full 6 miles (9.7km) away (which actually managed to fool some eager Spanish military archivists). Even Mexican revolutionary leader Pancho Villa got hip to the hype of film and offered to let the Mutual Film Corporation cover his campaign. But after the filmmakers discovered that the hero was also temperamental, they made the film without him and shot most of it in California instead of Mexico. Such was the fidelity of film.

As audiences adjusted to the medium, war movies—and film in general—grew by fits and starts. Movies had already grown in length. The industry standard had become a one-reeler—1,000 feet (305m) of film, which could run between ten and fifteen minutes, depending on the projector speed. Slowly but surely, the movies were also growing in vision. Increasingly, they relied on fictional stories rather than flatly filmed events to hold audiences' interest. Unfortunately, saccharine romance and unimaginative adventuring were often the order of the day. Gallant officers, frightened maidens, country bumpkins, secret agents—everyone was getting into the act as America edged toward World War I. War's full dramatic, sociological, and box-office potential had yet to be captured.

This book is your tour of duty through the very best of what's been fought out on film since the beginning. We'll heed the battle cry (the birth of talkies) and fight our way through four major international wars and a lifetime of cultural evolution. With marching orders from headquarters (MGM, Universal, Warner Brothers, and Columbia studios), we'll make our invasion by air (lofty and unusual films—even cartoons—hat you may not know of), sea (great productions in big trouble), and land (rock-solid classics that broke box-office records).

So prepare to be dropped behind enemy lines—into producer's offices—and wade into the action-packed Hollywood studios and exotic location sets. Get ready to hunker down in the trenches with stabled screenwriters, savor sensational skirmishes between headstrong actors and draconian directors, witness sacred alliances such as that between the War Department and the studios, and read mail from the home front (shifting public sentiment). Gear up and keep your head down. We're going in.

Chapter One

BEHIND THE SCENES WITH THE BIG GUNS

War may be hell, but it sells at the box office.

—director Robert Aldrich

Victor Fleming gives Scarlet O'Hara (Vivien Leigh) some last-minute marching orders before she sweeps down the stairs on the Tara set for Gone With the Wind *(1939).*

By 1909 director David Wark "D. W." Griffith (1875–1948) had become king of the one-reelers, cranking out more than 140 films for the Biograph Company in that year alone. True to his heritage as the son of Confederate colonel "Roaring Jake" Griffith, D.W. had also marshaled a tremendous staff around him. Instead of doing it all himself, from story and camera to direction and editing—as the great pioneer Edwin S. Porter had—Griffith delegated whatever duties he could, leaving himself free to tell one hell of a story.

Plot and acting were some of the factors that Griffith valued most. As a former playwright and stage actor, he knew how vital they could be to a film. By yanking the medium out of its long, drowsy, static scenes and using what we now call cross-cutting (cutting quickly back and forth from the main scene to any one of a number of other locations and actions), Griffith created a dynamic new reality that went beyond the scene onscreen and built dramatic tension that riveted viewers to their seats. He also livened up individual scenes by cutting from one character's perspective to another's (a process called shot-countershot) and by using close-ups that directed an audience's focus and emphasized character emotion. Like so many other filmmaking tools, these two devices are now taken for granted, but moviegoers should remember that these tools were created and honed by this one man—a man who was waiting for one passionate (though ill-conceived) film to take out his entire tool kit and get down to the serious business of filmmaking.

THE BIRTH OF AN ART FORM

In Turin, Italy, Giovanni Pastone had tapped into history with *Cabria* (1914), an unbelievably ambitious eighteen-reel operatic love story set during the Rome-Carthage wars of 300 B.C. Griffith also yearned to make a big film, a long film, an important film that would elevate his cherished medium to its rightful place in the artistic pantheon. He found it in the stage adaptation of the Reverend Thomas Dixon's two novels, *The Clansman* and *The Leopard's Spots*. Griffith shared Dixon's bitterness about what Reconstruction had done to the South. But the Baptist minister from North Carolina was also a bigot, and the story Griffith embraced for filming was overflowing with racism.

The Clansman follows the lives of two noble families—the Stonemans and the Camerons—as the Civil War tears them apart and forces them to take sides. Amid battle scenes and personal tragedies, this novel squeezes in decisive moments from the conflict, such as Lincoln's assassination at Ford's Theater and Sherman's fiery march through Atlanta. It also treats the war's sordid aftermath, complete with well-intentioned politicians, carpetbaggers, a lustful mulatto lieutenant governor, freed slaves out to deflower white womanhood, and a mighty, rescuing Ku Klux Klan.

Griffith had gotten into the habit of filming back east in the summers and in California for the winters. When Biograph balked at tackling such a large project, he cut ties with the company and took his stable of actors and his adventurous cameraman, Billy Bitzer, to Los Angeles.

In California, he went where no American film director had ever gone before: into extensive rehearsal. Griffith and company rehearsed for six weeks—which was unheard of in the two-film-a-week frenzy of his Biograph days. They even rehearsed in the rainy season so as not to waste days of useful light. Though Griffith and writer Frank E. Woods had come up with a story outline, most of the detail was still in Griffith's head. The cast, which included the young Lillian Gish, was kept unaware of the plot (a method that modern masters such as Federico Fellini have used to keep actors "acting in the moment"). Younger members of the company developed scenes while the older actors who would play them looked on before stepping into the roles.

On Independence Day, 1914, they started filming, mostly in the rural San Fernando Valley. A great deal of money was raised—more than five times the budget of any previous picture—and it was spent everywhere. An army of five thousand extras and the huge production crew had to be paid. Period artillery and explosives had to be bought. The town of Piedmont, South Carolina, had to be replicated. Atlanta was built only to be burned down. Four college professors were hired to research the period (though the lithographs in *Harper's Pictorial History of the Great Rebellion* ultimately inspired most of the sets). West Point engineers were hired to reproduce the Battle of Petersburg. Ford's Theater was duplicated in loving detail, except for the roof.

Some two hundred seamstresses worked for two months to make historically accurate costumes—12,000 yards (10,973m) of cloth were used on the women's dresses, and 25,000 yards (22,860m) of white sheeting went into making KKK costumes. For the climactic Klan ride to the rescue, the entire southwestern portion of Whittier County was rented—at a cost of $10,000 a day—and the inland route to Mexico was effectively closed. Night photography gobbled up $5,000. And real artillery shells were detonated during the battle scenes (where, if you look closely, you'll find Union and Confederate trenches set in the exact same place)—at a cost of $80 a pop.

This director would have done his daddy proud. For the battle scenes, which ranged over a 2-mile-long (3.2km) set, Griffith erect-

> *I cannot imagine a human emotion that is not included somewhere in this story.... One comes from this film saying: "I have done the South a cruel injustice, they are all dead, these cruelly tried people, but I feel now that I know them as they were; not as they ought to have been, but as they were; as I should probably have been in their place."*
>
> **—from the original program for *The Birth of a Nation***

No, they're not trick-or-treaters — they're the sheet-wrapped savages of the KKK in what may be the most influential war movie of all time, David Wark Griffith's **The Birth of a Nation** *(1915).*

ed a 100-foot (161km) observation tower. From there, he had field telephones running to operators placed every 50 yards (46m) along the field's perimeter. An army officer transmitted Griffith's orders for troop movement and artillery explosions to the appropriate operators, who in turn communicated to the troops in the field using flags, couriers, and even signal mirrors.

After nine weeks of shooting, three and a half months of editing, and $110,000 spent, he had the cinematic event of the young century. In Los Angeles, *The Birth of a Nation* ran for thirty weeks, and in New York it broke records at forty-four weeks. The first American film to warrant an intermission, it was so popular that it boasted two showings a day and the first reserved seats (at a cost of $2 per ticket). It grossed a record $18 million. Within the first six

months of the national run, this movie had been seen by more people than had gone to all the stage plays in the country during any five-year period.

The critics scrambled for superlatives. What else could they do with a film that President Woodrow Wilson (Dixon's old college chum) had called "history written in lightning"? But not everyone felt the way program writer Rupert Hughes did. Black Americans certainly didn't. Not when the depictions of them were derived not from historic renderings but from bestial political cartoons of the

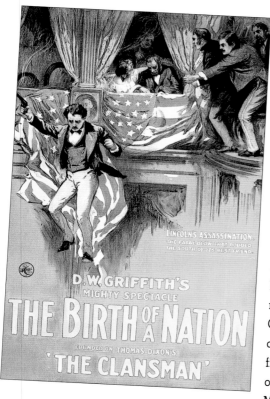

Reconstruction era. Not when the Atlanta premiere of the film included twenty-five thousand real marching, riding, shooting, Klansmen, whose organization had been pulled out of blessed obscurity and revived with the success of the film.

The NAACP flatly condemned *The Birth of a Nation*. Boston and Paris banned it. The film sparked race riots in New York, Chicago, Philadelphia, and other major cities where the film was screened. A review of the film published in the March 20, 1915, issue of the *New York Evening Post* quoted one New Yorker as putting identification with the film in a slightly different light: "That show certainly does make you hate those blacks. And if it gets that effect on me, when I don't care anything about it, imagine what it would be in the South, with a man whose family was mixed up in it. It makes you feel as if you'd do the same thing."

Responding to pressure, Griffith cut more than 150 of the most inflammatory shots, largely from the Reconstruction section. At the same time, however, he asserted his right to free speech and published the following letter: "I am not now nor have I ever been 'anti-Negro' or 'anti' any other race. My attitude toward the Negroes has always been one of affection and brotherly feeling. I was partly raised by a lovable old negress down in old Kentucky, and I have always gotten along extremely well with the Negro people."

Popular though he was, Griffith didn't have the final say. The United States Supreme Court got the last word on the controversy stirred by this great and greatly misguided film: "The exhibition of motion pictures is a business, pure and simple. Not to be regarded as part of the press of the country or as organs of public opinion. They are mere representations of events, of deeds and sentiment published and known, vivid, useful and entertaining no doubt, but as we have said, capable of evil, having power for it the greater because of their attractiveness and manner of exhibition."

An art form had been born. American war had been captured with amazing popular success. Film's chilling power for social propaganda was recognized. And the full-length Hollywood feature had made its debut. All other combat epics would just be chips off the old blockbuster.

This frozen leap from the balcony of Ford's Theater (John Wilkes Booth trying to escape after shooting you-know-who) graces a poster for Griffith's classic.

THE COMBAT FILM TAKES OFF

In its wake, World War I left almost nine million people dead and twenty thousand wounded. It also left Europe shattered and instilled in most moviegoers a general distaste for war films. Despite this feeling, former aviator Rex Ingram momentarily dazzled audiences in 1921 with his spectacular *Four Horsemen of the Apocalypse*. This tale of an adulterous Franco-Argentine (Rudolph Valentino in his film debut) spurred to patriotism by the sight of his lover's sightless husband returning from the trenches was brilliant in its imagery and vivid in its battle scenes. Although its popularity put Metro-Goldwyn-Mayer (MGM) on the map, it wasn't until film's old rival, theater, had tested the waters that war films got their next boost. In 1924, Maxwell Anderson and Lawrence Stalling's *What Price Glory* became a surprise Broadway hit. MGM saw the dollar signs and recognized the show's potential for equal success as a film. They bought the rights to the play and turned it into Raoul Walsh's 1926 film of the same name, then hired Stallings to write film's first intimate look at the American fighting: King Vidor's 1925 classic, *The Big Parade*.

With *The Big Parade*'s big box-office returns, Hollywood was encouraged to put its combat gear back on. The next big war film was made by another former flyer, and this time it was about aviation. In 1926, William (later known as "Wild Bill") Wellman was a director of little experience, especially when it came to war pictures. He did have experience of war, however—he had served with the Lafayette Flying Corps, an offshoot of the fabled Lafayette Escadrille, in World War I.

One cold, gray morning in February 1926, famed aviation instructor John Monk Saunders pitched a war story set against the untouched "Kingdom of the Sky" to Paramount studios producer Jesse Lasky in the library of his New York apartment. Lasky was intrigued. Saunders' story of two friends who are romantic rivals and fellow flyers had a great deal of dramatic potential—especially when the average life of a World War I combat pilot in the air was a mere forty-eight hours—and represented new territory for motion picture cameras to explore. The cost, however, seemed prohibitive—at least until Saunders flew to Washington, D.C., to enlist the financial support of Secretary of War Dwight F. Davis. With money matters solved, Lasky was sold. And Wellman, with his experience and ambition, was the natural choice to direct.

Wings (1927)—one of the last truly great silent pictures—took off in grand style. The military gave production a home at Camp Stanley in San Antonio, Texas, as well as the loan of a staggering $16 million worth of equipment and manpower. Tanks, trucks, and wire poured in from Fort Sam Houston. Balloon officers, crew, and equipment came in from Scott Field in Illinois. The 2nd Engineers Company dug trenches. The 2nd Signal Company wired up a telephone network. The 2nd Ordinance Company took on explosives work. The 8th Armored Corps provided soldiers, guns, and artillery. Camp Stanley itself was converted into a French battlefield under the supervision of General Paul B. Malone at a cost of $300,000.

For battle sequences, Wellman had twenty-one cameramen set up to catch action from a multitude of angles. Some were perched atop 100-foot (30.5m) towers, others were masked on the sidelines, and still others were dug down in the dirt. However, the air was where Wellman worked his magic. Army pilots of the First Pursuit Group formed the core of his flying personnel. Trick pilots added their expertise, and the two male stars pitched in a little as well—Richard Arlen had been a member of the Royal Flying Corps during the war and Buddy Rogers had flown in the navy. When it came to planes, civilian planes were often used in place of military ones. Although a few real De Havilland DH4s were used, Thomas Morse MB3 Scouts masqueraded as Spads, Curtis P-1s passed for Fokkers, and Massive Martin Bombers played the German Gotha Bombers.

The risks they took were real—there was one army casualty during filming—because the flight and action sequences were real. There were no special effects, and no studio process was used to trick the film up—except for a little blue tinting for the flight sequences and red bursts for machine-gun fire.

Long shots were best for capturing the high-speed dogfights. But shooting could be held up for weeks at a time while Wellman waited for the right background mix of sun and clouds. If there was too much blue sky, the planes lost their scale, looking like "goddamn flies" to Wellman. Sometimes the best backdrop was the ground below.

Because every inch of film was precious, two planes were squeezed into a single frame whenever possible. Two men to a plane was also the rule. Stars were often housed in two-seater planes—the actor sat up front and the actual pilot sat in the rear. Remote-controlled cameras were welded, behind the cockpit over the pilot's shoulder, and even on the wings and landing gear. In one ten-plane dogfight staged at 12,000 feet (3,658m), one of the best pilots in the country was paid to take a 6,000-foot (1,829m) tailspin with the camera rolling directly at his face all the way down.

In theaters, these incredible aerial scenes were projected in Magnascope (a forerunner of Panavision, today's widescreen aspect), and management often added backstage sound effects of engines and machine guns. Audiences went wild. *Wings* won the first Oscars ever for best picture and best special effects, was one of the first films to be novelized, and became the source of stock footage for the flock of flying pictures it inspired. With a success like this, the sky was the limit for Hollywood war movies.

To those young warriors of the sky whose wings are folded about them forever, this motion picture is reverently dedicated.

—original program dedication for *Wings* (1927)

A tense moment down in the dugout, waiting for the shelling to begin again in King Vidor's The Big Parade *(1925).*

YOU AIN'T JUST WHISTLIN' DIXIE!

As a child, southern belle Peggy Marsh had injured her ankle in a bad riding fall. Reinjury in 1926 as an adult left the $25-a-week journalist stuck in her Atlanta apartment while her ankle healed. Her husband, an advertising executive, suggested that she pass the time writing some kind of little book. She decided to work on a story about the Civil War. Starting with the last chapter first, she scribbled notes describing one Rhett Butler walking out of the doors of Fontenoy Hall as Pansy O'Hara loses her last chance at love.

After four laborious (more than seventy drafts of chapter one alone), erratic, and highly secretive years of writing, Peggy's not-so-little book had gone through numerous title changes, from *Bugles Sang True* to *Tote the Weary Load* to *Tomorrow Is Another Day*. The book was finally released, under the pen name of Margaret Mitchell, as *Gone With the Wind*, and it took the United States by storm, selling 176,000 copies in its first month of publication. The rights were snapped up by Hollywood mogul David O. Selznick for a record $50,000.

SCRIPTING: TOMORROW IS ANOTHER DRAFT

Even though Mitchell didn't want to have anything to do with writing the screenplay from her book, lots of other writers did, and many of them got the chance—for a few minutes anyway. Pulitzer Prize–winning playwright Sidney Howard was first up; in six weeks, he cranked out a four hundred-page behemoth that would have run six hours (Selznick's office had figured that filming the entire book would have resulted in a 168-hour film).

When Howard finished, the exhausted playwright returned to Massachusetts to take care of business at his 700-acre (283ha) cattle farm. Later, Joe Swerling, who would go on to collaborate in the creation of *Guys and Dolls* (1950), took a crack. Playwright Oliver H.P. Garrett labored under Selznick's directive to add no more than one hundred lines of dialogue to those existing in Peggy's book. John Van Druten, author of the plays *I Remember Mama* (1944) and *Bell, Book and Candle* (1950) had his try, as did Charles MacArthur, coauthor of *The 20th Century* (1932) and *The Front Page* (1928), and six other eminent American writers, including F. Scott Fitzgerald.

Finally, famed literary gun Ben Hecht accepted $15,000 to sequester himself for a week with Selznick and then-director Victor Fleming to create a workable script from Howard's original monster. His role was script writer as secretary—he wrote the scenes as Fleming and Selznick acted them out for him (now there's a Rhett and Scarlett duo to have watched in action). The three commonly worked for eighteen to twenty-four hours at a stretch, and Selznick eliminated all distractions. For some reason, he decided that even real food was a distraction, and the trio fueled themselves only on bananas and peanuts (although Hecht also popped uppers).

After five frenzied days, Selznick collapsed while eating a banana. On the sixth day Fleming burst a blood vessel in his eye and Hecht bailed. Only half the script was finished.

Selznick soon recovered and confidently took over the second half. When he floundered, he again called Sidney Howard, who finished the screenplay under Selznick's watchful and meddlesome eye. With the script complete, Howard again returned to Massachusetts. Being the perfectionist he was, Selznick probably would have called on Howard again, but before long the playwright was tragically crushed in a tractor accident.

TOMORROW IS ANOTHER DEAL

From the start, everyone wanted box-office king Clark Gable for Rhett Butler (except Mitchell, who wanted Basil Rathbone). Gable, however, wanted nothing to do with the part. He didn't think he had the talent, and he didn't think Rhett fit his macho image. MGM's chief executive, Louis B. Mayer (Selznick's father-in-law), offered him up anyway—in exchange for distribution rights and a hefty percentage of the gross. Gable might have been able to withstand the pressure if he hadn't needed money—lots of money. To marry his lover, actress Carole Lombard, Gable first had to pay off his estranged wife. Selznick created pressure by asking the wife's lawyer, a friend of his, to keep the squeeze on. Mayer added more leverage by threatening to end Gable's contract if he didn't take the role, at the same time promising to pay the $400,000 divorce settlement for him if he did. Gable yielded.

Leslie Howard, who was always cast as the refined, sensitive, dashing, well-spoken Englishman (*Of Human Bondage*, 1934, and *The Petrified Forest*, 1936), was just as reticent. At the age of forty-nine, he was tired of playing Romeos (a film role he had had to play at the tender age of forty-six) and yearned to be on the other side of the camera. Selznick and Mayer wooed him with promises of associate-producing an upcoming production of *Intermezzo*. With this bribe, he accepted the role of the tragically sensitive and aristocratic Ashley Wilkes (Scarlett's other man).

TOMORROW IS ANOTHER AUDITION

Thanks to Selznick's tremendous publicity campaign and the novel's immense popularity, the part of Scarlett O'Hara (as Pansy had been renamed by the time Mitchell created her final draft) was the most coveted and controversial role of the century. When Selznick found that established actresses weren't quite right for the role, he initiated a nationwidetalent search at a cost of $92,000—during which fourteen hundred candidates were interviewed and ninety tested, and thirteen thousand feet (3,962m) of pricy Technicolor film were shot.

Florence Nightingale she's not. Still, Scarlet is slowly waking up to smell the chicory among the thousands of wounded in **Gone With the Wind** *(1939).*

Good Christ, we could never make this picture, it would cost a fortune!

—Vice President in Charge of Finance Henry Ginsberg to producer David Selznick after having just read Margaret Mitchell's novel *Gone With the Wind*

Thousands of women from all over the United States and Europe wrote in offering to take the role of Scarlett. Socialites from all over the South, including William Randolph Hearst's wife (Patty Hearst's mother), interviewed for the part. So many actresses marched into Selznick's office that his driveway was renamed "Scarlett Way." One enterprising young woman even leaped out of a packing crate in Selznick's office and proceeded to strip in front of him while quoting lines from the novel. Another emerged in full antebellum costume from a book-shaped Christmas box delivered to his home. Even Margaret Mitchell was rumored to be in training at MGM to take on the role.

As almost everyone knows, it was Vivien Leigh who finally played the notorious southern belle, but many other actresses—celebrated and unknown—were in the running.

BETTE DAVIS was the first choice, but when she was paired with Errol Flynn (an early contender for the part of Rhett), she flatly refused and went off to do her own southern belle in Jezebel (1938). Overaged TALLULAH BANKHEAD wanted the part, but she was unbankable because of her legendary life of debauchery. Still, her politically powerful Alabama family launched a statewide campaign to petition Hollywood on her behalf. NORMA SHEARER's name was leaked to columnist Walter Winchell to test the public waters, but Mitchell thought the actress was too dignified. Later, Shearer claimed that the part she really wanted was Rhett. The mature KATHERINE HEPBURN was briefly considered—Selznick quipped that she had a hard-to-photograph face that was one-half angel and one-half horse. PAULETTE GODDARD, though a great kisser in her screen test with Leslie Howard's Ashley, was the kiss of death because of her prenuptial life in sin with the left-leaning Charlie Chaplin. Besides, Chaplin wanted her to remain available for his first talkie (which is covered later in this book).

And the list goes on: JOAN CRAWFORD, LANA TURNER, MIRIAM HOPKINS, JOAN FONTAINE, SUSAN HAYWARD, and even LUCILLE BALL were all considered, and each of them passed. No one, however, could quite match the face that Mitchell had so specifically etched in her novel: "In her face were too sharply blended the delicate features of her mother, a coast aristocrat of French descent, and the heavy ones of her Irish father. But it was an arresting face, pointed of chin and square of jaw. Her eyes were pale green without a touch of hazel, starred with bristly, black lashes and slightly tilted up at the ends. Above them, her thick black brows slated upward, cutting a startling oblique line in her magnolia white skin."

TOMORROW IS ANOTHER SET

It wasn't until Atlanta was in flames that David Selznick found his Scarlett. With time running out on Gable's availability and dollars dripping away, Selznick decided to start the picture even though he still didn't have a leading lady or a decent script. He had been warned to use models to re-create Sherman's burning of Atlanta, but decided instead to lay contiguous sprinkler pipelines through the more than 30 acres (12ha) of old, tinder-dry sets in Culver City, California. Two pipelines were ready to spew a highly flammable solution of 80 percent distilled oil and 20 percent rock gas. A third ran water and extinguishing solution to keep Culver City from going up in flames. If things went right, Selznick would have a fire scene to end all fire scenes and 30 acres of clear land to build new sets on.

All of the world's seven Technicolor cameras were in place to record the conflagration on later matte shots behind crowd scenes. Three pairs of Scarlett and Rhett stunt doubles were poised for action. So was every fire department in the Los Angeles area, braced to hose burning bits of debris out of the air. Selznick was perched above it all on a tower, mastering the controls.

WOULD YOU BELIEVE THAT...?

- *Selznick had two versions of Rhett's last lines filmed: the much-quoted version and "Frankly, my dear, I just don't care," just in case the Motion Picture Code censors did give a damn.*
- *The crafty film crew sewed 70 pounds (31.8kg) of lead weights into the hem of Olivia De Havilland's skirts and stood by for the scene where Gable had to lift her up in his arms.*
- *The first director, George Cukor, gave De Havilland some offscreen impetus during her birthing scene by reaching underneath the bed sheets and twisting her ankle.*
- *The second director, Victor Fleming, quit after arguments with Leigh over his making Scarlett look like a "bitch." Before stalking off the set, he rolled up his script and screamed, "Miss Leigh, you can stick this script up your royal British ass!"*
- *Dialect coach Susan Myrick used the following line to instill southern flavor in accent-deficient Gable and Howard: "Ah cain't offoad a foah doah Fohd."*
- *Twenty-five hundred extras were requested on such short notice for the famous crane shot of the field hospital scene that one thousand dressed dummies had to supplement fifteen hundred actors, who rocked the mannequins to make them look barely alive.*

During the burning, which was started and stopped eight times, Selznick's brother, an agent named Myron, stopped by with some dinner guests to watch the fun. One of them was married to his client Laurence Olivier (who himself would star the next year in a film borrowing the fire footage, Rebecca). She had been raised in India and schooled in England, Switzerland, Germany, and France. Like Scarlett, one parent was French (distantly) and the other Irish. Getting his brother's pyromaniacal attention, Myron turned Selznick so he could see the firelit face of Vivien Leigh, saying, "Here, genius. I want you to meet Scarlett O'Hara." The rest, as they say, is history.

P.O.W. SPELLS POW!!!

We've all been taken hostage by prisoner-of-war movies. Fighting on the front lines is bad enough, but waiting out the war in a state of deprivation, exhaustion, and often torture, risking almost certain death to escape, and selling your soul to stay alive is a hell all its own. Like combat, the P.O.W. experience tests what a man is made of. Of the scores of P.O.W. films that have been made, one stands out as the most praised, most decorated, and even the most devious ever to "captivate" an audience for two hours.

David Lean's *The Bridge on the River Kwai* (1957) was adapted from a story written by real-life P.O.W. Pierre Boulle. In this tale, a proper British colonel named Nicholson surrenders to the Japanese in the jungles of Burma, only to face a supreme contest of wills with his prison camp commandant, the equally unequivocal Colonel

> The first time, I didn't like the script; second, I thought it was anti-British; third, I just didn't like the role.
>
> —Sir Alec Guinness on Colonel Nicholson and *The Bridge on the River Kwai* (1957)

Saito, over the issue of building a bridge across the River Kwai to serve a Japanese army railway that will run from Singapore to Rangoon.

Kept captive in Camp 16, where "[t]here is no barbed wire, no stockade, [and] no watch tower," just impenetrable Siamese jungle and no chance of escape, Nicholson's stubborn refusal to have his officers serve as laborers earns him weeks of torture, which come to an end only when he negotiates for them to supervise construction of the bridge. Confident that engineering and building a proper British bridge will boost his men's morale, Nicholson attacks the project with a nationalistic fanaticism that outstrips even that of his captors. But when an American GI named Shears manages to escape, he is sent back to destroy the symbolic bridge.

ME TARZAN. YOU HIMMLER.

Just who fought the good fight in Hollywood movies? You might be surprised.

RANGE DEFENDERS (1937)
Brown-shirted goons with SS-style armbands oppress Western citizens on the range.

SOUTH OF THE BORDER
(1939) *Singing cowboy Gene Autry battles Nazis who want to set up a submarine base on the coast of Mexico.*

CHARLIE CHAN IN PANAMA
(1940) *The "inscrutable" sleuth busts up a spy ring in the Canal Zone.*

RIO RITA (1942) *Abbott and Costello star in an update of a Broadway musical in which Nazi agents make radios in the form of apples on a Texas ranch.*

SHERLOCK HOLMES AND THE VOICE OF TERROR (1942)
A mysterious radio voice in London broadcasts saboteur activity, and the great sleuth (who is some-how stillalive in the 1940s) enlists the help of a cockney prostitute and her Limehouse cronies to unmask the culprit.

TARZAN TRIUMPHS (1943)
Nazis overrun a jungle utopia called Polandria (sounds a touch familiar, no?) and abduct Boy. Cheetah masquerades as the Führer on the telephone. And Tarzan (Johnny Weismuller) utters the wise words, "Jungle people fight to live; civilized people live to fight."

His name may be Weismuller, but don't let it fool you. He's a regular guerrilla when it comes to fighting Nazis in the patriotic **Tarzan Triumphs** *(1943).*

The Bridge on the River Kwai is so permeated by bravery, honor, and patriotism that it's only after being swept along that you begin to realize that its message is the madness and futility of war. In fact, the making of the movie bordered on madness. Trekking 10,000 miles (16,093km) away from Hollywood to an abandoned stone quarry in Ceylon (which looked more exotically Siamese than Siam), the cast and crew battled 120°F (49°C) temperatures (sunstroke felled an average of four people a day), finger-size leeches that had to be burned off with cigarettes or salt, and an unruly mob of extras (thirty-seven nationalities that included large numbers of Ceylonese juvenile delinquents called Bambalawatta boys) who so severely stampeded the set during a parachuting scene that it had to be scrapped from the picture.

Alec Guinness, who played the majestically misguided Nicholson (the portly Charles Laughton, the producers' first choice, later conceded, "I never understood the part until I saw Guinness play it"), faced numerous dangers. These included almost being crushed by a falling tree, having to deal with a pink-eared elephant with a blood clot that needed constant massage throughout the shoot, and receiving a bloody nose after being slapped by an overzealous Colonel Saito (former silent star Sessue Hayakawa). Guinness strode through all these with his good nature and typical British aplomb; after being struck by Hayakawa, he quipped that he was "bleeding for his art."

Unlike the real bridge, which had been quickly sketched on cigarette paper and smuggled out to Lord Louis Mountbatten's

Such a pretty bridge—and so much work (eight months of Ceylonese labor)—it seems a shame to blow it up. But that's just what director David Lean did at the climax of his WWII epic, **The Bridge on the River Kwai** *(1957).*

Southeast Asia headquarters, the movie version's was cost-elaborate. It cost one-twelfth of the entire $3 million budget lavished on the production by producer Sam Spiegel. It was more than 130 yards (119m) long and 50 feet (15.2m) high and took a full eight months to build. But the expense didn't end with the construction. Spiegel bought a train and six coaches from the Ceylonese government railway to be driven over the bridge. He had 100 acres (40.4ha) around it cordoned off to protect civilians from flying debris. Then he sent five cameras and crews inside the protected area—in tanks, pillboxes, concrete dugouts, and sandbagged trenches—and blew up the bridge with 7,000 pounds (3,175kg) of TNT.

The explosion remains one of the most hair-raising and ironic climaxes that ever graced a movie. And Spiegel knew it would be—he was so nervous about losing the phenomenal footage that he gave it a police escort from the jungle to the airport and flew it to London for processing in five separate planes (in case one of them crashed or was hijacked). The result of all the plotting and pyrotechnics was a stunning seven-Oscar sweep at the Academy Awards, all backing up the producer's boast, made during production, that "this picture is so authentic that the Ceylon government has asked us to acknowledge the fact that the picture was shot under peacetime conditions."

AND BEHIND SIMILAR ENEMY LINES...

See if you can match up the stars with the P.O.W. pictures they starred in.

STAR

1. Spencer Tracy evades Nazi captors
2. Duke rescues Quinn from "Death March"
3. Dana Andrews after Doolittle raid on Tokyo
4. Ol' Blue Eyes steals a Nazi train
5. Sly Stallone makes soccer game escape
6. Brian Keith chases Nazi prisoners through the heather
7. The Cooler King and pals tunnel to freedom
8. Ex-president learns about North Korean brainwashing
9. Newman's own kind of Korean collaborator
10. Karl Malden's directorial debut
11. Wallace Beery snagged by submarine
12. Rin Tin Tin fetches flyer from the Hun
13. Hopalong Cassidy captive
14. Flyboy Moriarty downed in Vietnam
15. Hackman makes it a family affair
16. This time Sly kicks butt
17. You can't ignore Norris
18. Holden's heroic heel finds a spy
19. Segal's wheeler dealer

FILM

A: Time Limit *(1957)*
B: The Purple Heart *(1944)*
C: Von Ryan's Express *(1965)*
D: Back to Bataan *(1945)*
E: The Seventh Cross *(1944)*
F: Victory *(1981)*
G: Thunder Afloat *(1939)*
H: The Arabian Knights *(1927)*
I: Dog of the Regiment *(1927)*
J: Prisoner of War *(1954)*
K: King Rat *(1965)*
L: The Great Escape *(1963)*
M: The Rack *(1956)*
N: Stalag 17 *(1953)*
O: Missing in Action II: The Beginning *(1985)*
P: The McKenzie Break *(1970)*
Q: The Hanoi Hilton *(1987)*
R: Rambo: First Blood, Part II *(1985)*
S: Uncommon Valour *(1983)*

Williamson (Michael Moriarty) saying "welcome to hell" to the newest P.O.W. to be a guest at **The Hanoi Hilton** *(1987).*

Answers
1=E, 2=D, 3=B, 4=C, 5=F, 6=P, 7=L, 8=J, 9=M, 10=A, 11=G, 12=I, 13=H, 14=Q, 15=S, 16=R, 17=O, 18=N, 19=K.

THE WAR COMES HOME

These sentiments didn't seem to matter to the protest-conscious Pentagon and War Department. These offices had been helpful in funding, supplying, and aiding scores of films that delivered approval of World War II and the Korean conflict, but in regard to Vietnam they had virtually closed their coffers and consultants to all but John Wayne's gung-ho production of *The Green Berets* (1968). Nevertheless, in 1978 one director managed to get his surprisingly uncritical and humanizing message through. No matter how badly he bombed making the $36 million debacle of *Heaven's Gate* (1980) and no matter how many times Mickey Rourke's hair changed color in *Year of the Dragon* (1985), Michael Cimino should always be revered as the first man who found a way to successfully translate the agonizing American loss of innocence in the Vietnam War to the big screen.

The Deer Hunter (1978) is about three working-class buddies who join the army together in 1968 and the devastating effects the war has on them as well as the people around them in the steel town of Clariton, Pennsylvania. Like a religious triptych of epic scale and loving detail, this saga follows the lives of Michael (Robert De Niro), Nick (Christopher Walken), and Steven (John Savage). They go together from a sweet hometown life filled with hard work, weddings, deer hunts, boozing, bonding, and wide-eyed patriotism through the living hell of combat and captivity with the Viet Cong, which leaves Michael a hero, Steven a cripple, and Nick insane. They return home to pick up the pieces of life, friendship, and stateside community in the wake of what they've been through.

Cimino had been a medic with the Green Berets in Vietnam as well as an architecture student at Yale, a director of television commercials, and a writer on such films as *Silent Running* (1971) and *Magnum Force*. While some critics later complained that he whitewashed American involvement and demonized the enemy, he spared no expense (out of a then-colossal $12 million budget) in making every other aspect of the film as real as possible.

To begin with, there was the town of Clariton, Pennsylvania, which Cimino made as real and as American as apple pie. Eight different cities in four different states were used to create this illusion. While the entire town of Mingo Junction, Ohio, was "autumnized" for a midsummer shoot, $25,000 was spent on fabricating the bar owned by John Welch (George Dzundza), where the boys shoot pool while lip-synching "Goin' Outa My Head Over You."

Months of negotiations and a $5 million insurance bond were needed to convince U.S. Steel to allow filming to take place—for the first time ever—on the floor of their central blast furnace in Cleveland, Ohio. There, in proximity to blistering 3,000°F (1,649°C) temperatures and covered in asbestos from head to foot, De Niro, Walken, Savage, the weaselly John Cazale, and bearish Chuck Aspegren "tapped" molten steel by hand. It was a process normally and more safely done by drill, but Cimino wanted to emphasize the teamwork needed in the time period.

In the inferno, Robert De Niro, himself no stranger to meticulous detail, insisted on keeping sight lines as free of crew members as possible so that his concentration would not be affected. The actor had spent six weeks before the start of production tramping through the Ohio River Valley, talking and drinking with mill hands, dining in their homes, and recording their speech patterns. As he said, "I go through all of this so I can feel I've prepared as well as I can. It's my job. I want to feel I've earned the right to play a person."

After seven solid weeks of earning that sweaty right, Cimino, the stars, master cinematographer Vilmos Zsigmond, and the crew flew to Bellingham, Washington, to spend three weeks shooting the almost mythically beautiful deer-hunting sequences atop

ABOVE: Robert De Niro bides his time in the tiger cages of the Viet Cong, just before a game of Russian roulette, in Michael Cimino's heartfelt **The Deer Hunter** *(1978). OPPOSITE: Director Cimino and costars De Niro and Streep in conference during the filming of* **The Deer Hunter.**

10,000-foot (3,048m) Mount Baker. After only two days off, they embarked for Thailand for the grueling Vietnam sequences. To prepare for their scenes, the boys watched a tape created by production consultant Joann Carelli, who sifted through ten years' worth of Vietnam footage supplied by NBC, ABC, and CBS to come up with a two-hour crash course on the Vietnam War.

Schedule-delaying and budget-bloating monsoons began only hours after the company's production schedule had been posted in Thailand. The civilian-led government, which had pressured the United States to remove all its military bases and personnel in March 1976, was slow to accommodate the American group with support and supplies. But all that changed when a "revolutionary party" led by military leaders staged a coup d'état on October 6, 1976—Cimino and company found themselves in the thick of it in the Katchanaburi district of northwestern Thailand, near the Burmese border.

Fears of the junta bringing a halt to his filming—or doing something far worse—proved unfounded, as the new government not only provided Cimino with all the military equipment he needed, but also posted one heavily armed guard for every three crew members to protect the crew from a camp of insurgents only 93 miles (150km) away. Cimino and company worked twelve hours a day, six days a week to finish the film and get out of harm's way. This tension can only have added to the stars' legendary Russian

roulette scene, which New York magazine critic David Denby called "the most hair-raising ten minutes in the history of American movies."

And as if all that weren't stressful enough, after a swaying bamboo bridge had been built across the 40-foot-wide (12.2m) River Kwai (not far from the site where the famed bridge had spanned the waterway), both De Niro and Savage insisted on performing their own stunts, dropping 30 feet (9.1m) from a rescuing helicopter into the swiftly moving waters below—for fifteen takes.

Back in Bangkok, Cimino violated a citywide curfew and wrangled six thousand extras as he filmed for another two hectic nights on that city's Tu Do Street, re-creating the decadent chaos of Saigon's Patpong Road (a/k/a "Street of a Thousand Pleasures"). Again, the tension in civilians and filmmakers alike no doubt added a certain realism to the desperate scene.

The Deer Hunter swept up five Oscars and made Cimino one of the biggest overnight successes since Orson Welles. It's ironic to think that the tearful relief of the final scene, where the shattered group of friends reconvenes at the bar to sing "God Bless America" (set to a haunting classical guitar arranged and performed by John Williams), must have been filmed long before the earlier scenes of overseas hardship had even begun. There would be so many more reasons for laughter and tears in the weeks and months ahead.

THE MIRACLE

Sometimes great war movies are not about combat; once in a while, the subject is a different kind of fight. Sometimes the heroes of a war movie are anything but typical. Sometimes we realize that an infamous event shown on film again and again has never really hit home.

> He who saves one life, saves the entire world.
>
> —the Talmud

One of the most momentous films of recent times was born from a seemingly trivial moment. Australian writer Thomas Keneally (*The Chant of Jimmy Blacksmith*, 1978) was passing through Los Angeles on his way back from a film festival in Italy when he decided to go to Beverly Hills and buy a new briefcase. While he was chatting with shop owner Leopold Poldek, Keneally let it slip that he was a writer. Poldek told him that he had the best story of the century. Keneally was skeptical until Poldek identified himself as a concentration camp survivor and said, "I was saved by a big, good-looking Nazi named Oskar Schindler. Not only was I saved from Gross-Rosen, but my wife, Mila, was saved from Auschwitz itself. So far as I'm concerned, Oskar is Jesus Christ. But though he was Jesus Christ, he wasn't a saint. He was all-drinking, all-black-marketeering, all-screwing." Keneally started taking notes to put in his new briefcase.

As Keneally began to research Oskar Schindler and his rescue efforts, he found that Poldek and his wife were not the only lucky ones. In Poland, Nazi party member, cunning industrialist, pathological philanderer, and wartime profiteer Oskar Schindler had somehow managed to save twelve hundred Jewish men, women, and children from extermination by claiming them as indispensable employees in his enamelware factory. To save these people, he had bribed, bluffed, and bargained. He had befriended one of the Nazis' most sadistic commandants, Amon Goeth (who set dogs on children to watch them torn apart and had lashing recipients who didn't keep count of their strokes lashed all over again). He had rescued three hundred women from Auschwitz after they had been rerouted there while on their way to his labor camp. And in the seven months that his factory was operational, it produced nothing that was of any value to the German army. At war's end his employees, who came to call themselves *Schindlerjuden* ("Schindler Jews"), inscribed that term in a ring for him that they had made with the gold from their own teeth, helped him escape the German-hunting Russians, and eventually (when his postwar adventures bankrupted him) brought him to Israel. Keneally used

Oskar doesn't look like the kind of guy who'd save the lives of twelve hundred Polish Jews, but looks can be deceiving — especially if you're Liam Neeson in Steven Spielberg's Schindler's List *(1993).*

his research to write a stirring novel that seemed to beg for a movie treatment.

Steven Spielberg had wanted to film an adaptation of Keneally's holocaust novel since making *E.T.* (1982), but had lacked the time, confidence, and clout to do it for a full ten years. After completing the filming of *Jurassic Park* (1993), Spielberg, spurred by the atrocities being committed in Bosnia—which seemed to echo the horrors of Nazi Germany—decided that it was finally time to film the story of Oskar Schindler and those he rescued. He admits now that he would never have had the stomach for the carefree carnage of *Jurassic Park* if he had made *Schindler's List* (1993) first.

Not only did Spielberg plan to shoot his $23 million, three-and-a-quarter-hour Holocaust film in black and white, he originally wanted to record the soundtrack in German and Polish and provide English subtitles. The studio executives at Universal begged him to shoot in color and transfer the film to black and white afterward, but Spielberg hung tough and mollified them by promising not to ask a dime for himself until the studio had made its $23 million investment back at the box office. He won the color battle but lost the language argument.

Spielberg cast Irishman Liam Neeson as the charismatic Schindler and gave the actor home movies of his late mentor, the former Time-Warner head Steve Ross, to study for an expressive, expansive physicality. For Goeth, Spielberg cast thirty-one-year-old British actor Ralph Fiennes, whom he had seen in a BBC version of *Wuthering Heights*. Fienne tested so well on the first of his three takes that Spielberg never bothered to view the second two. Part of Fiennes' preparation for the role was gaining 28 pounds (12.7kg) to attain the paunchy sadist's girth.

Spielberg made his own metamorphosis. In a later interview, he reflected that "the reason I came to make the movie is that I have never in my life told the truth in a movie. My effort in movie making has been to create something that couldn't possibly happen."

For Spielberg, creator of so many fantasy films, honesty became the new policy. Principal photography began in Poland on March 1, 1993, during which time Spielberg oversaw editing of *Jurassic Park* via satellite. Scenes of Oskar Schindler's real apartment building and factory were possible in Kraków because that city had been spared major devastation in Allied bombings. To get at the truth and "pull the events closer to the audience," Spielberg "reduced the artifice," stripping his technique of many of the tools he had come to use so well. He canceled crane orders. He tore up dolly track. Eventually, a full 40 percent of the footage was created using a handheld camera.

Schindler's labor camp, complete with thirty-four barracks, seven watchtowers, and a main road paved with Jewish tomb-

> *I've got a pretty good imagination. I've made a fortune off of my imagination. My imagination is dwarfed by the events of 1940 to 1945, just dwarfed. And so I couldn't imagine the Holocaust until I went to Kraków, and to Auschwitz-Birkenau for the first time.*
>
> **—Steven Spielberg**

stones, was reconstructed according to plans of the original. With the help of local Poles, who donated countless pieces of period clothing, costumer Anna Sheppard had to design and assemble more than eighteen hundred costumes for the thirty thousand extras involved in the project.

While the local government did not allow Spielberg to shoot on the actual grounds of Auschwitz, the enterprising filmaker did spend two eerie days shooting just outside its fences. Special bald caps that covered both the neck and the head had to be created for close-ups of concentration camp women. Some effects were as real as blood itself. Like the prisoners they played, who needed to rouge their sallow cheeks to look healthy enough to work (the policy in the concentration camps was work or die), several female cast members pricked their fingers and used their own blood for coloring.

The subject matter and the realism took their toll. An elderly woman who had been a prisoner of the real Amon Goeth visited the set and almost fainted from fright after seeing Fiennes in his Nazi finery. At the replica of Goeth's villa, erected less than a mile (1.6km) from the original blood-soaked site, Spielberg, who had hired German actors to play some of the minor Nazi roles, found himself being hostile to them while they were in uniform. There were few shenanigans on these sets. When things were at their most grimly resonant, the director found himself calling his friend Robin Williams to say, "I haven't laughed for seven weeks. Help me, here!" And Williams would proceed to do twenty minutes of stand-up on the phone to Poland.

After seventy-two days of filming (four days less than projected in the schedule), Spielberg finished what many consider his masterpiece—and Hollywood's most important film in decades. *Schindler's List* garnered thirteen Oscars, and as of August 1995 it had grossed more than $320 million at box offices around the world. Spielberg has poured his profits from this film directly into his *Shoah Project*, a massive film chronicle of personal Holocaust narratives. Though banned in countries like Egypt, Indonesia, and Jordan, *Schindler's List* has brought the barely acknowledged atrocities of the Holocaust to light in Russia, where it has spurred the release of *The Black Book*, a Soviet film on Nazi genocide that had been banned since Stalin's time for "political errors." Most important, Spielberg's film has been a humanitarian wake-up call to hundreds of thousands of American teens and preteens. And the director has provided screenings and lectures for many youngsters at his own expense. He has said that his goal is to open the eyes of six million young souls—a number with resonance when it comes to the Holocaust. This is one blockbuster that has made an impact far beyond the box office.

THE VICTORS!

It may not be the Iwo Jima statue, but that little gold guy makes a lot of heads (especially studio heads) snap to attention. Let's look at some of the war-related features that have taken home Hollywood's most distinguished decoration.

1927/1928
Best Picture and Engineering Effects (Roy Pomeroy): **Wings;** *Best Actor (Emil Jannings):* **The Last Command**

Clara Bow with Buddy Rogers and Richard Arlen in Wings *(1927).*

1928/1929
Best Interior Decoration (Cedric Gibbons): **The Bridge of San Luis Rey**

1929/1930
Best Picture and Director (Lewis Milestone): **All Quiet on the Western Front**

1930/1931
Best Original Story (John Monk Saunders): **Dawn Patrol**

1932/1933
Best Picture and Director (Frank Lloyd): **Cavalcade;** *Best Cinematography (Charles Bryant Lang Jr.) and Sound Recording (Harold C. Lewis):* **A Farewell to Arms**

1935
Best Director (John Ford), Actor (Victor McLaglen), and Score (Max Steiner): **The Informer;** *Best Assistant Director (Clem Beauchamp and Paul Wing):* **Lives of a Bengal Lancer**

1939
Best Picture, Actress (Vivien Leigh), Supporting Actress (Hattie McDaniel), Cinematography (Ernest Haller and Ray Rennahan), Interior Decoration (Lyle Wheeler), Film

Editing (Hal C. Kern and James E. Newcom), and Director (Victor Fleming): **Gone With the Wind**

1941
Best Actor (Gary Cooper) and Film Editing (William Holmes): **Sergeant York;** *Best Special Effects (Photographic—Farciot Edouart and Gordon Jennings; Sound—Louis Mesenkop):* **I Wanted Wings**

1942
Best Picture, Actress (Greer Garson), Supporting Actress (Theresa Wright), Director (William Wyler), Cinematography (Black and White—Joseph Ruttenberg), and Screenplay (George Froeschel, James Hilton, Claudine West, and Arthur Wimperis): **Mrs. Miniver;** *Best Actor (James Cagney), Sound Recording (Nathan Levison), and Score of a Musical Picture (Ray Heindorf and Heinz Roemhold):* **Yankee Doodle Dandy**

1943
Best Picture, Director (Michael Curtiz), and Screenplay (Julius J. Epstein, Philip G. Epstein, and Howard Koch): **Casablanca;** *Best Actor (Paul Lukas):* **Watch on the Rhine;** *Best Supporting Actress (Katina Paxinou):* **For Whom the Bell Tolls;** *Best Film Editing (George Amy):* **Air Force;** *Best Special Effects (Fred Sersen):* **Crash Dive**

1944
Best Score for a Drama (Max Steiner): **Since You Went Away;** *Best Special Effects (Photography—A. Arnold Gillespie, Donald Jahraus, and Warren Newcombe; Sound—Douglas Shearer):* **Thirty Seconds over Tokyo**

1945
Best Scoring of a Musical Picture (George Stoll): **Anchors Aweigh**

1946
Best Picture, Actor (Fredric March), Supporting Actor (Harold Russell), Director (William Wyler), Screenplay (Robert E. Sherwood), Film Editing (Daniel Mandell), and Score for a Drama or Comedy (Hugo Friedhoffer): **The Best Years of Our Lives;** *Best Actress (Olivia De Havilland):* **To Each His Own**

1949
Best Supporting Actor (Dean Jagger) and Sound Recording (20th Century Fox Sound Department): **Twelve O'Clock High;** *Best Screenplay (Robert Pirosh) and Cinematography (Black and White—Nicolas Vogel):* **Battleground**

1951
Best Actor (Humphrey Bogart): **The African Queen**

1953

Best Picture, Supporting Actor (Frank Sinatra), Supporting Actress (Donna Reed), Director (Fred Zinneman), Cinematography (Black and White—Burnett Guffey), Sound Recording (Columbia Sound Department), and Film Editing (William Lyon): From Here to Eternity; Best Actor (William Holden): Stalag 17

1955

Best Supporting Actor (Jack Lemmon): Mister Roberts Best Special Effects (Photographic—Paramount Special Effects Department): The Bridges at Toko-Ri

1957

Best Picture, Actor (Alec Guinness), Director (David Lean), Screenplay Based on Material from Another Medium (Pierre Boulle—pseudonym for Carl Foreman and Michael Wilson), Cinematography (Jack Hildyard), Film Editing (Peter Taylor), and Music Scoring (Malcolm Arnold): The Bridge on the River Kwai; Best Supporting Actor (Red Buttons), Supporting Actress (Miyoshi Umeki), Art Direction (Ted Haworth), and Sound (Warner Brothers Sound Department): Sayonara

1958

Best Sound (Todd-AO Sound Department): South Pacific

1959

Best Supporting Actress (Shelley Winters), Cinematography (Black and White—William C. Mellor), and Art Direction (Black and White—Walter M. Scott and Stuart Reiss; Set Decoration—Lyle R. Wheeler and George W. Davis): The Diary of Anne Frank; Best Picture, Actor (Charlton Heston), Supporting Actor (Hugh Griffith), Cinematography (Color—Robert L. Surtees), Film Editing (Ralph E. Winters and John D. Dunning), Sound (MGM Sound Department), Art Direction (Color—William A. Horning and Edward Carfagno; Set Decoration—Hugh Hunt), Scoring of a Drama or Comedy (Miklos Rozsa), and Costume Design (Elizabeth Haffenden): Ben-Hur

1960

Best Supporting Actor (Peter Ustinov), Cinematography (Color—Russell Metty), and Art Direction (Color—Alexander Golitzen and Eric Orbom; Set Decoration—Russell A. Gausman and Julia Heron): Spartacus

1961

Best Actor (Maximilian Schell) and Screenplay Based on Material from Another Medium (Abby Mann): Judgment at Nuremberg; Best Actress (Sophia Loren): Two Women; Best Special Effects (Visual—Bill Warrington; Audible—Vivian C. Greenham): The Guns of Navarone

1962

Best Picture, Director (David Lean), Cinematography (Color—Fred A. Young), Sound (Shepperton Studio Sound Department), Film Editing (Anne Coates), Art Direction (Color—John Box and John Stoll; Set Decoration—Dario Simoni), and Music Score Substantially Original (Maurice Jarre): Lawrence of Arabia; Best Black and White Cinematography (Jean Bourgoin and Walter Wottitz): The Longest Day

1965

Best Screenplay Based on Material from Another Medium (Robert Bolt), Cinematography (Color—Freddie Young), Art Direction (Color—John Box and Terry Marsh; Set Decoration—Dario Simoni), Music Score Substantially Original (Maurice Jarre), and Costume Design (Color—Phyllis Dalton): Doctor Zhivago

1967

Best Foreign Language Film: Closely Watched Trains (Czechoslovakia)

1968

Best Foreign Language Film: War and Peace (U.S.S.R.)

1970

Best Picture, Actor (George C. Scott), Director (Franklin J. Schaffner), Story and Screenplay (Francis Ford Coppola and Edmund H. North), Sound (Douglas Williams and Don Bassman), and Film Editing (Hugh Fowler): Patton; Best Screenplay Based on Material from Another Medium (Ring Lardner Jr.): MASH; Best Special Effects (Visual—A.D. Flowers and L.B. Abbott): Tora! Tora! Tora!

1971

Best Foreign Language Film: The Garden of the Finzi-Continis (Italy)

1978

Best Picture, Supporting Actor (Christopher Walken), Director (Michael Cimino), Sound (Richard Portman, William McGaughy, Aaron Rochin, and Darrin Knight), and Film Editing (Peter Zinner): The Deer Hunter; Best Actor (Jon Voight), Actress (Jane Fonda), and Screenplay (Story—Nancy Dowd; Screenplay—Waldo Salt and Robert C. Jones): Coming Home

1979

Best Cinematography (Vittorio Sotaro) and Sound (Walter Murch, Mark Berger, Richard Beggs, and Nat Boxer): Apocalypse Now; Best Foreign Language Film: The Tin Drum (Federal Republic of Germany)

ABOVE: The face of courage: Denzel Washington as fugitive slave turned crack fighting man in Edward Zwyck's Glory (1989). BELOW: The face of cowardice: Klaus Maria Brandauer is the actor who sold his soul to the Third Reich in Istvan Szabo's chilling Mephisto (1981).

1981

Best Director (Warren Beatty), Supporting Actress (Maureen Stapleton), and Cinematography (Vittorio Sotaro): Reds; Best Foreign Language Film: Mephisto (Hungary)

1982

Best Supporting Actor (Louis Gossett Jr.), Original Song ("Up Where We Belong": Music—Jack Nitszche and Buffy Sainte-Marie; Lyrics—Will Hennings): An Officer and a Gentleman

1983

Best Supporting Actress (Linda Hunt): The Year of Living Dangerously

1984

Best Supporting Actor (Haing S. Ngor), Cinematography (Chris Menges), and Film Editing (Jim Clark): The Killing Fields

1986

Best Picture, Director (Oliver Stone), and Film Editing (Claire Simpson): Platoon; Best Foreign Language Film: The Assault (Netherlands)

1989

Best Director (Oliver Stone) and Film Editing (David Brenner and Joe Hutshin): Born on the Fourth of July; Best Supporting Actor (Denzel Washington), Cinematography (Freddie Francis), and Sound (Donald O. Mitchell, Gregg C. Rudolf, Elliot Tyson, and Russell Williams II): Glory; Best Costume Design (Phyllis Dalton): Henry V

1991

Best Foreign Language Film: Mediterraneo (Italy)

1992

Best Foreign Language Film: Indochine (France)

1993

Best Picture, Director (Steven Spielberg), Cinematography (Janusz Kaminski), Screenplay Based on Material Previously Produced or Published (Steven Zallian), Film Editing (Michael Kahn), Art Direction (Color—Allan Starski; Set Decoration—Ewa Braun), and Original Score (John Williams): Schindler's List

Chapter Two

THE DOGFACES

They weren't heroic figures as they moved forward one at a time, a few seconds apart. You think of attackers as being savage and bold. These men were hesitant and cautious. They were really the hunters, but they looked like the hunted. There was a confused excitement and a grim anxiety in their faces. They seemed terribly pathetic to me. They weren't warriors. They were American boys who by mere chance of fate had wound up with guns in their hands, sneaking up a death-laden street in a strange and shattered city in a faraway country in the driving rain.

—combat reporter Ernie Pyle in a July 13, 1944, newspaper column

Oh he's five foot two and he's six feet four,
He fights with missiles and with spears,
He's all of thirty-four and he's only seventeen,
Been a soldier for a thousand years

—from "The Universal Soldier," by Buffy Sainte-Marie

Tough-as-nails Sergeant Stryker (John Wayne) will have to be just that as he and his dogfaces wait for the next attack of the "Japs" in The Sands of Iwo Jima *(1949).*

DOUGHBOY HISTORY 101

Never underestimate them. Alexander the Great didn't. They conquered the known world for the grasping Greek in only eleven years (334–323 B.C.). A little more than a hundred years later, thirty thousand of them (along with horses and elephants) helped a Carthaginian general named Hannibal give Rome a run for its money by pouring across Spain, slogging over the Alps, and marching into Italy and on to where all roads lead. The well-paid and highly organized Roman Legionnaires reciprocated by sacking Carthage fifty years later in the Third Punic War, establishing the dominance of their short broadsword and shield for the next five hundred years. Only when the fallen Roman Empire's infantry got whipped by hordes of eastern barbarians in A.D. 378 did the foot soldier take a backseat to the horseman. And that ride was only for a thousand years or so.

In 1415, English archers equipped with the far-reaching longbow gave French knights a drubbing at the Battle of Agincourt. The tables turned even more against horsemen with the increasing boom of guns and gunpowder. In the seventeenth century, when the musket and the pike became the weapons of choice, large, well-organized, and well-trained foot soldiers were the backbone of European armies. This backbone was more bone than brain, however. Thanks to Frederick II of Prussia, foot soldiers were little more than synchronized feet attached to guns—living, moving, fighting, and dying in a solid block.

The French Revolution of 1789 successfully nationalized the idea that citizens with a cause made better and more reliable soldiers than did mercenaries, whose motivation was profit. This idea of citizenry being converted into an organized militia had been advocated by Florentine mastermind Nicolò Machiavelli in the 1500s and put into practice by King Gustave II Adolph of Sweden in the 1600s. And it was perfectly suited to the freedom-fighting Americans of the 1700s.

The colonists had learned a thing or two from their tribal neighbors while fighting the French and Indian Wars, even if the English troops hadn't quite gotten the message. Those guerrilla tactics stood the patriots in good stead as they hid from and pounced on advancing lines of paid dragoons.

The increased killing power of combat in the American Civil War, complete with its introduction of barbed wire, grenades, and repeating rifles, called for higher and higher levels of infantry organization and discipline. With the dawn of the twentieth century, technology, quick and reliable train transport, assembly line–produced trenching tools, and machine guns were the order of the day—and the modern foot soldier had a lot to keep in mind besides the glory of battle.

THE PARADE COMES TO TOWN

With the large-scale combat and carnage of World War I, the old, gentlemanly rules of war saw their last light. Fighting men began to take some of the emphasis off personal honor and did more team playing with their increasingly organized military units. Some apsects of combat were still waged with the elitist bonhomie ("Curse you, Red Baron!") so notable in European wars of old. However, the men who died in the trenches came from all walks of life. In America, with widespread conscription ushered in by the Selective Services Act of 1917, men were putting down their pitchforks, fountain pens, sledgehammers, and polo mallets and standing shoulder to shoulder to fight the good fight.

Screenwriter and playwright Lawrence Stallings had lost his left leg in World War I. In the early 1920s, Stallings' *What Price Glory* was running on Broadway. After MGM producer Irving Thalberg saw this play about war, he asked Stallings to write a short story for him. The result was the glamourless five-pager "The Big Parade," whose major themes were realism and commonality. Thalberg took the story and made it into the film of the same name.

A ROSE BY ANY OTHER NAME WOULD STILL SMELL AS SWEET

Over the centuries, there have been a lot of terms used to describe the average infantryman, both young and old. Here are just a few of the monikers that have stuck to the beloved dogface—some distinctly more dignified than others.

Bing boy (Canadian)
Digger (Australian)
Doughboy (an American allusion to the large, globular glass buttons on Civil War infantry uniforms)
Footslogger
GI (short for "government issue")
Grunt
Janissary (Turkish)
Kanonenfutter (German for "cannon fodder")
Lady from hell (Scottish)
Man-at-arms
Old campaigner
Poilu (French)
Sepoy (Indian)
Serviceman
War horse
Tommy Atkins (British)
Trooper

The Big Parade (1925) tells the story of three enlisted American soldiers at the French front (not surprisingly, no part of the film was actually shot in France): a tobacco-chewing riveter named Slim (Karl Dane), a beefy bartender named Bull (Tom O'Brien), and James Apperson, the society son of a southern mill owner (John Gilbert, risking his matinee-idol image). These three pals march off to war together in a breathtaking sequence that gives the film its name. They eat, sleep, ride the train, brawl, and shovel manure together. They even fall for the same feisty French farmer's daughter, Melisande (Renée Adorée), who not only has the cutest learning-to-chew-gum scene you'll ever see, but actually gets dragged from a troop truck when she cannot bear to leave the GI she's fallen for. At the front, they heroically pit themselves against an enemy machine-gun nest—two of them die and the third is forced to crawl through no-man's-land sharing a last cigarette with the German sniper he's just shot, before heading for the hospital, home (minus a leg), and heroic disillusionment.

Director King Vidor told Thalberg that he wanted to make a substantive film that "comes to town and stays longer than a week." He put his all into making sure that this first important Hollywood film about the Great War would also be the first to look seriously at the life of the common soldier. True, it was released almost ten years after the war had ended, but as Vidor said:

It would take ten years to evolve a true war picture. Propaganda and the passions of the struggle blind the participants from seeing it sanely; the satiety and a cynical reaction follow, no less blinding and distorting.

Heartthrob John Gilbert seems to be doing a little throbbing of his own thanks to the adoring gaze of Renée Adorée in The Big Parade (1925).

Vidor wanted realism—most of the time, anyway. He spent hours viewing War Department footage. In sequences just before combat, he noticed troops marching at a cadence that was eerily and ominously slow. He slowed his screen soldiers down to the same dreadful beat. To gauge the pace of fighting, he set a metronome to a low tempo and ordered a drummer to beat out the pace of battle scenes. Every death movement was done to the sound of the drum. Although one extra (a British veteran) asked Vidor if he was staging "some bloody ballet," the effect was moving.

To further ensure authenticity, Vidor hired two ex-soldiers as technical advisers. When he discovered that a German workman on the set had actually seen an occupied German machine-gun nest, Vidor made him an adviser as well, and even gave him a part. He bucked MGM by having his hero return legless, instead of just limping home as the executives had originally planned.

It's ironic that this gritty film had perhaps its most profound effect on the American painter Andrew Wyeth. Years later, Wyeth claimed to have run the film 188 times. He said he was inspired by its realism—especially the love scene among plowed French fields—to paint *The Summer of 1942* and *Snow Flurries*. Hearing this, Vidor went to the now urbanized Westwood, Los Angeles, location where he had shot the scene and took a bubble-bursting photograph of the "French fields," which he sent to Wyeth with a note that said, "That's what happened." As realism went, the illusion had been pretty good.

ARMYWOOD

In the early forties, isolationists were claiming that many of Hollywood's war films—particularly the paranoiac *Confessions of a Nazi Spy* (1939) and the shining true story of the pacifist-turned-soldier-extraordinaire, *Sergeant York* (1941)—were sheer propaganda created with the intent of edging the United States into World War II. Although other films, like the army- and navy-pilot-preparedness movies *Flight Command* (1940), *Dive Bomber* (1941), and *I Wanted Wings* (1941), had been less inflammatory, in the autumn of 1941 the Committee on Interstate Commerce started an investigation to find out if filmmakers were indeed teaming up with politicians to sway public sentiment. In December of that year, a day that would live forever in infamy erased all complaints. After the surprise attack at Pearl Harbor, the United States joined the war, fighting in the European and Pacific theaters, and the Hollywood movie machine got squarely behind the American war machine and joined hands with the propagandizing Office of War Information.

The equation was simple. The armed forces needed Hollywood to make war pictures that would boost American morale and encourage enlistment by depicting the services in a favorable light (especially the navy, which had very little presence in America's land-locked heartland). But Hollywood would not make movies just for its country's sake. Although the towers of Tinseltown were filled with patriotic sons of immigrants, the movie industry was first and foremost a business that set its sights on the bottom line. The U.S. government understood. Washington donated advisers, extras, vehicles, man-power, equipment, and locations —all of which would slim down bulging budgets— and war pictures consequently got an enthusiastic thumbs up from studio heads.

Even so, it was a little while before the armed forces could provide much material help for moviemakers. Assessing and filling the need for manpower and supplies at the front took precedence over propaganda. With the horror of Pearl Harbor and the successive Pacific theater losses of Wake Island, Guam, British Malaya, Singapore, the Dutch East Indies, Thailand, and the Philippines from late 1941 through 1942, war movies had to show the heroism behind the brutal hardship of war.

Hollywood films optimistically portrayed heroes surviving incredible peril. In the celebrated *Air Force* (1943), directed by Howard Hawks, the motley crew of the *Mary Anne* (a B-17 Flying Fortress)—including John Garfield, Harry Carey, Arthur Kennedy, and Gig Young—just misses the massacre at Pearl Harbor, squeaks in to refuel at a besieged Wake Island (rescuing a doomed pooch named Tripoli to be their mascot), manages a perilous 7,000-mile (11,265km) flight to the collapsing Philippines (where they perform several dangerous missions), and then decimates the Japanese fleet (made of miniatures and bombed in Santa Monica Bay at a cost of $500,000) on their way to Australia to prepare for the aerial assault on Tokyo. In real life, however, soldiers were seldom so lucky or so mobile.

Many of these soldiers of the Good War were fighting in circumstances of certain death. During the forties, the focus of movies set against the backdrop of World War II was eased away from

dashing, star-driven exploits and onto the trials and triumphs of the mixed units of regular GIs and the rugged men who led them. The marines, desperately holding on to Wake Island in December 1942, were heroes to be remembered —and martyred. In *Wake Island* (1942), the filmic story of these heroes, director John Farrow and screenwriters W.R. Burnett and Frank Butler, using marine corps records and with material assistance from the War Department, established the formula for hundreds of heroic-soldier-team movies to come.

Trapped on a speck of land in the Pacific with a flotilla of Japanese battleships and squadrons of Japanese planes closing in, a stoic group of entrenched soldiers waits, trading wisecracks and patriotic wisdom as they prepare for their final stand. (The film was actually shot in the arid wastes near California's Salton Sea using miniature ships and planes.) There's the rugged commanding officer with a soft spot for his men (Brian Donlevy), the surly salt from the heart of Brooklyn (William Bendix), the self-sacrificing hero with a great big chip on his shoulder (McDonald Carey), and the fast-talking city boy (Robert Preston). All fight courageously in the face of doom.

Fighting men (and women), Hollywood style.
OPPOSITE, TOP: Ray Milland (left) and young William Holden take a publicity break with Veronica Lake in I Wanted Wings (1941). OPPOSITE, BOTTOM (left to right): Walter Pidgeon, Ruth Hussey, and Robert Taylor strike a slightly more serious pose for Flight Command (1940). ABOVE: In the true and terrible story of Wake Island (1942), Robert Preston and William Bendix play two marines who plan to fight against all odds.

In 1943, director Tay Garnet returned to the team theme with the classic *Bataan*. A reworking of the plot of John Ford's 1934 World War I desert picture, *The Lost Patrol*, *Bataan* chronicled the lives and deaths of a single patrol of army dogfaces facing overwhelming odds after Japan's December 1941 invasion of the Philippines. Trying to hold on to one last corner of the mountainous Bataan Peninsula just west of Manila Bay by guarding a bridge they've

just blown, the patrolmen hope to buy time for the retreating General Douglas MacArthur to prepare a counteroffensive. Tragically, by late February, President Franklin D. Roosevelt had ordered MacArthur to leave the conquered islands, which he did, vowing, "I shall return." The unlucky thirteen men in the company do not go with him.

Visionary MGM production chief Dory Schary wanted to commemorate their sacrifice while waking up the moviegoing public to the rough road ahead. With no military assistance (though the Office of War Information loved the result, especially the fact that it portrayed commanding officers listening to their subordinates), the sweltering action was filmed entirely on soundstage 16, in what Garnet called a "real-as-hell jungle with everything except 16-foot [4.9m] snakes." It certainly looked real enough to audiences unspoiled by location jungle shoots. Sweat dripped, ghostly moonlight beamed, shot men jerked their bodies around to emulate death throes (and received sprained ankles and wrists, thanks to the jerking of unseen ropes), and ground fog crept eerily (almost killing two extras crawling through its dry-ice fumes).

Bataan offers not only glory and sacrifice, but an ethnic twist on the team theme, provided by a vivid ensemble of (slightly stereotyped) characters. The members of this cross section of army

A bandaged Desi Arnaz (center) listens to something much more riveting than "Babaloo" as CO Robert Taylor and the boys (including Japanese-American and Filipino soldiers) look on in Bataan *(1943).*

society lose their lives one by one, until the last defiantly takes on what seems like the entire Japanese infantry—after first digging his own grave. There's a music-loving Mexican from Los Angeles (Desi Arnaz), a gutsy Filipino ex-boxer (Roque Espiritu), a navy hayseed who writes his mother regularly (Robert Walker), a crusty New Yorker named Feingold with an Irish brogue (Thomas Mitchell), a Pole from Pittsburgh (Barry Nelson), a moral reprobate who redeems himself in blood (Lloyd Nolan), and, of course, the gruff sergeant (Robert Taylor) who grudgingly takes command.

Schary had asked writer Robert Andrews to leave one of the characters racially unspecified. In this role, Schary cast black actor Kenneth Spencer as demolition expert Wesley Epes. Breaking the Hollywood-military color barrier drew lots of flak, but *Bataan's* gritty group was a big hit with the public. So big, in fact, that John Wayne himself starred in *Back to Bataan* (1945)—a portrayal of the brutal 65-mile (104.6km) death march in which twenty-five thousand Allied prisoners died on the way to the Japanese-held Camp O'Donnell.

GOLDEN ODES TO THE COMMON MAN

All through World War II and even into the fifties, hundreds of war pictures showed supermanly men making the heroic best of a bad situation or training other men to do so. They even made real war heros like twenty-four-time-decorated Audie Murphy into real movie stars. In director Zoltan Korda's *Sahara* (1945), for instance, Humphrey Bogart kept five hundred thirsty Germans away from a precious water hole in North Africa. This time, the cast was multinational, including both upper- and lower-class Brits, a South African, a Frenchman, a Sudanese soldier, an Italian prisoner, and a downed German pilot. For this one, the army supplied equipment and sent five hundred GIs in German uniforms to serve as extras and perform desert maneuvers at the location 100 miles (160km) east of Palm Springs. Army personnel also contributed to veracity by strafing the desert to show the cinematographer what machine-gun bullets kicking up sand looked like.

Still, not all war pictures pictured larger-than-life patriots leading supernaturally spunky soldiers into the glory of war. The very best showed combatants as credible common men. Just after the war had ended, one film wowed audiences by painting an unpretentious, almost documentary portrait of the American GI and what he had been up against. Many moviegoers (including General Dwight D. Eisenhower) considered it the best movie to come out of World War II. *The Story of G.I. Joe* (1945) was based on two books by the Pulitzer Prize–winning war correspondent Ernie Pyle: *Brave Men* and *Here Is Your War*. (Although Pyle was just a middle-aged newshound, he was the favorite of the GIs, over such luminaries as Ernest Hemingway, John Steinbeck, John Dos Passos, and John Hersey.) The movie follows the roving reporter (Burgess Meredith as Pyle) as he falls in with what the real Pyle called his "mud-rain-frost-and-wind boys"—members of the 18th Infantry's Company C (including Robert Mitchum as Lieutenant Walker) fighting their way from Sicily to Rome in 1942 and 1943.

When producer Lester Cowan decided that it was time to bring Pyle's words to the screen, his first choice to direct was John Huston. When Huston didn't pan out, Cowan decided to try William "Wild Bill" Wellman. Unfortunately, Wellman wanted nothing to do with it—he was an ex-flyer and maintained the flyer's disdain for the ants below. The stalwart producer, however, was not one to give in easily, and he embarked on a campaign to draft Wellman as directorial commander in chief.

Cowan walked into Wellman's house uninvited, pitched him the story, was politely refused, persisted, and was chased out of the house with Wellman yelling that he was "not going to work his ass off for infantry!" Cowan returned a few days later with Pyle, only to have the door slammed in his face before an introduction could be made. A few days later, he returned again with gifts for all of Wellman's kids (whom he knew by name). Wellman told him to stay away or he'd put him in the hospital. Pyle finally telephoned Wellman personally. Wellman later admitted that Pyle's pleas for the common soldier were so eloquent that Wild Bill was almost brought to tears. Pyle convinced the hardcase to visit him at his Albuquerque ranch, and there Bill was won over.

Wellman crafted an austere, documentary-style film with off-screen matter-of-fact narration by Meredith. (A former army private and air force captain, Meredith had written, produced, and acted in two training films of his own). *The Story of G.I. Joe* followed no plot except the flow of the featured soldiers' lives and deaths. No big sentimental strings were pulled. Detail (the privations of a Christmas in the elements), intimacy (a soldier's endless search for a phonograph to play a record of his son's voice), and honesty (when Walker is brought back dead on a mule, we aren't told how he died) are what make this movie great.

Wellman requisitioned 150 veterans of the army's Italian campaign to serve as his everyman extras and assigned some of them speaking parts. The relatively small number of actors in the picture were made to go through the same rigorous physical training that the soldiers underwent as they filmed, while the real McCoys enjoyed a little bit of Hollywood luxury and prepared to fight in the Pacific. When the film was finished, Wellman bid his "recruits" a fond farewell (he had become drinking buddies with a number of them). Tragically, many of his young pals were killed in the Pacific during the next year, as Pyle was himself in his continuing role as correspondent. *The Story of G.I. Joe* became the only one of his films that William Wellman refused to watch.

The following year, Burgess Meredith gave his narrative voice to a more grimly poetic paean to the common soldier. Framed with a gospel-style ballad, punctuated by a GI's internal letter to his sister, and filled with human moments and dark philosophizing rather than patriotic speeches, *A Walk in the Sun* (1946) proved that great grit can be arty, stylish, and even wordy when it needs to be. Lewis Milestone, who had directed the classic film adaptation of Erich Maria Remarque's *Im Westen nichts neues* (the English version appeared as *All Quiet on the Western Front*) in 1930, independently produced and directed Robert Rosen's script of ex-private Harry Brown's best-selling 1944 novel. In the end, Milestone came up with a work that was so enduring that it was one of the first films snapped up for television.

In *A Walk in the Sun*, Private Windy Craven (John Ireland) is huddled with his buddies on a landing craft about to hit the blood-

> *Look, you have a goddamn broken-down old flier who is going to be your boss. Now you just have to make up your mind that I'm a tough son-of-a-bitch. I want you to do exactly what I want you to do, but I'll never double-cross you…. When it's all over you'll see something up there that will be more than a picture of the infantry; it might just be a monument, and I am going to make it if it breaks my ass.*
>
> —director William Wellman to his army extras during the filming of *The Story of G.I. Joe* (1945)

drenched beach of Salerno, Italy. The night around him erupts in cannon blasts from shore (as the sounds of war pervade so much of this picture) as he speaks the letter he will never write:

> Dear Frances,
> I'm writing you this letter relaxing on the deck of a luxury liner. The natives have evidently just spotted us and are setting up a little reception: fireworks, music and that sort of stuff. Hah! The musicians in our own band have also struck up a little tune. Hah-hah! The gentle waters of Mare Nostrum. That's really good. Mare Nostrum.

As we have learned from the spiritual sung during the film's credits, an infantry platoon is about to take "a little walk in the

Italian sun." With all this sardonic understatement, you know it ain't gonna be no picnic. Their lieutenant is dead. Their commanding sergeant will crack up. Planes will strafe them, tanks will shell them, machine guns will mow them down, many will die. The short 6 miles (9.7km) from the beach through the woods to an occupied farmhouse and a bridge that must be blown up will be more like a walk through the valley of the shadow for these fifty-three souls, about ten of whom we will get to know intimately.

Like *The Story of G.I. Joe*, *A Walk in the Sun* is a superb slice of soldierly life (here reduced to one day) that brings together an ethnic mix of players who are from places as distant and disparate as the Old South and the South Bronx. Unlike Pyle's privates, however, these men voice eloquent and chillingly honest insights through

their dialogue. Sure, it's a little literary, but it's also straight from the heart.

The drawling, smoky-voiced medic, McWilliams (Sterling Holloway), complains, "We've got a grandstand seat, only we can't see nuthin'. That's the trouble with war, you can't see nothing! You have to find them by ear." Machine-gunner Rivera (Richard Conte) prepares to cover his troops with the confident yet self-mocking boast, "Nobody dies." He shares cigarettes and borscht-belt banter with his fellow New Yorker, Private Friedman (George Tyne), who doesn't want "a purple heart in the head." Unit scout Archimbeaux (Norman Lloyd) ponders when the endless war will reach Tibet. Former farmer Sergeant Ward (Lloyd Bridges) can't get apples off his mind. And a reluctant Sergeant Tyne (Dana Andrews) prepares himself for the onslaught that awaits them upon reaching their objective.

Talky as they are, these men rise to the grim and bloody occasions that meet them, again and again. They earn the right to make wisecracks, which seem as eloquent as the hurried soldier's grave (a helmet atop a rifle stuck bayonet-down in the sand) that Dana Andrews leaves for a fallen fellow on the beach. For a movie that sells itself as anything but noble, *A Walk in the Sun* stylishly earns its ad slogan: "The picture that captures the heart of our time—for all time."

The third in the triumvirate of classics featuring the World War II foot soldier was set in Belgium's frozen fields and woods. This return to *The Battle of the Bulge* paid tribute to "The Battered Bastards of Bastogne." Wellman must have whet his appetite for the infantry with *The Story of G.I. Joe*, because he didn't need coaxing—just "an awful lot of money"—to make *Battleground* (1949). This time, the heroes were, in Wellman's words, "a very tired group of guys": two U.S. paratrooper divisions who faced incredible odds holding on to a hub of seven intersecting highways that were vital to keeping open the Allies' supply line from Antwerp and to keeping America's army from being separated from Canadian and British forces.

By the time Eisenhower sent the 101st Airborne (the Screaming Eagles) to fill the vital gap in the Ardennes on December 18, 1944, the Eagles had already seen sixty-seven days of unbroken combat

OPPOSITE, TOP: *Burgess Meredith's (second from left) insightful portrayal of war journalist Ernie Pyle touched the hearts of millions of readers, viewers, and soldiers in* **The Story of G.I. Joe** *(1945).* **OPPOSITE, BOTTOM:** *Meet "The Battered Bastards of Bastogne," who face a wintry siege against incredible odds in one of the best war movies ever made, William Wellman's miraculous* **Battleground** *(1949).*

in Holland. By December 19, they were snowbound and fogbound; visibility was at zero, so no supplies (food, clothes, or ammo) could be dropped to them. By the twenty-first, they were encircled by twenty-five German armored divisions. By the twenty-second, the Nazis had given them an ultimatum to surrender, to which their commanding officer, Brigadier General Anthony C. McAuliffe, responded, "Nuts!" Together, they held off an enemy siege for more than a month of the coldest European winter in decades, until almost the last moment of survival. On March 15, 1945, General Dwight D. Eisenhower made history by giving the Distinguished Unit citation to the whole 101st Division.

Sergeant Robert Pirosh, though not at Bastogne, had fought with the 35th Division throughout the Ardennes. Before the war he had crafted screen comedies like the Marx Brothers' *A Day at the Races* (1937) and *I Married a Witch* (1942). Although he had vowed never to write a war movie, Pirosh took to the hard-boiled GI sense of humor. During Christmas week of 1944 he was sitting in a cold foxhole whistling "Silent Night" as German 88s screamed by overhead. As another one split the silence he gritted his teeth and muttered, "Incoming mail." His grim joke made even him laugh, so he scribbled it down. Soon he was jotting character sketches and observations of GIs carrying around precious eggs to cook in their helmets, big-footed country boys who liked to leave their boots outside the foxhole to give their feet a rest, snowball fights, and the baseball quizzes used to determine whether an unknown soldier was a Nazi spy.

When Pirosh returned to Hollywood, he pitched his story to producer Dory Schary, who had moved from MGM to RKO since the making of *Bataan*. The producer liked the story immediately, and he liked it even better when he found out that Pirosh had enlisted the support of the tough-talking McAuliffe to ensure story accuracy. But he wasn't sure that America was hungry for war pictures so soon after the Good War had ended. Americans hadn't been eager for them after World War I. He knew that patriotic appeal alone would not guarantee the success of this picture, but with the winning combination of humor and heroic hardship in Pirosh's script, he was willing to gamble. When Howard Hughes bought RKO and wanted Schary to scrap the project, the producer left the company and bought the rights for $20,000. *Battleground* would be his first picture back at his former home, MGM.

To prevent premature adverse reaction from the public and to deter competition from other studios, *Battleground* went into production incognito, disguised as a "psychological drama" called *Prelude to Love*. Wellman rankled at Schary's insistence on inserting a sermonizing message (appropriately delivered by a chaplain) and the addition of buxom French bombshell Denise Darcel, but he liked the script. To keep him happy, Schary had a wall knocked down between two soundstages, upon which the director could make a realistic mammoth winter battlefield. Except for the opening and closing sequences, even backgrounds would be simulated by projecting images from the rear onto screens placed on the set. The French villa set from *The Story of G.I. Joe* was resurrected and orders were placed for a lot of fake snow.

As in so many classic combat pictures, reality was the watchword during the filming of *The Story of G.I. Joe*. Pirosh went back to Belgium with a still photographer to record images of the countryside—they even found his old foxhole. The set was built using 520 trees shipped in from northern California and almost 500,000 feet (152,400m) of lumber for constructing mounds and hillocks. The army also got into the act, supplying official records, combat footage, stills, equipment, and men. Lieutenant Colonel Harry W.O. Kinnard, who had masterminded the resistance against the Nazi siege, became chief technical adviser. Twenty of the paratroopers who had helped him hold Bastogne were flown in from Fort Bragg to serve as extras.

Wellman had the soldiers buddy up one-on-one to rigorously train with cast members like star Van Johnson (whom Wild Bill goaded by constantly calling him Heflin), the tobacco-chewing James Whitmore, the denture-clacking Douglas Fowley, the venerable George Murphy, and the jovial Ricardo Montalban. Here is a sample daily schedule, military style:

0900–0950	Calisthenics
0950–1000	10-minute break ("Smoke 'em if you got 'em!")

ABOVE: Dana Andrews wonders just how long it will be before this shell-shocked soldier cracks in Lewis Milestone's poetic A Walk in the Sun (1946). OPPOSITE: Bruiser Wallace Beery indulges in the patriotic pastime of Nazi-strangling in Salute to the Marines (1943).

1000–1050	Learning firing positions—prone, sitting, kneeling.
1050–1100	Break
1100–1200	Scouting, patrolling, creeping, crawling, searching an area
1200–1300	Lunch
1300–1350	Grenade throwing, bayonet fighting
1350–1400	Break
1400–1450	Orientation film and lecture: "How to Get Killed in One Easy Lesson"
1450–1500	Break
1500–1550	Truck training—mounting, dismounting, bumpy truck
1550–1600	Break
1600–1700	Script rehearsal: Scenes 185, 187, 190

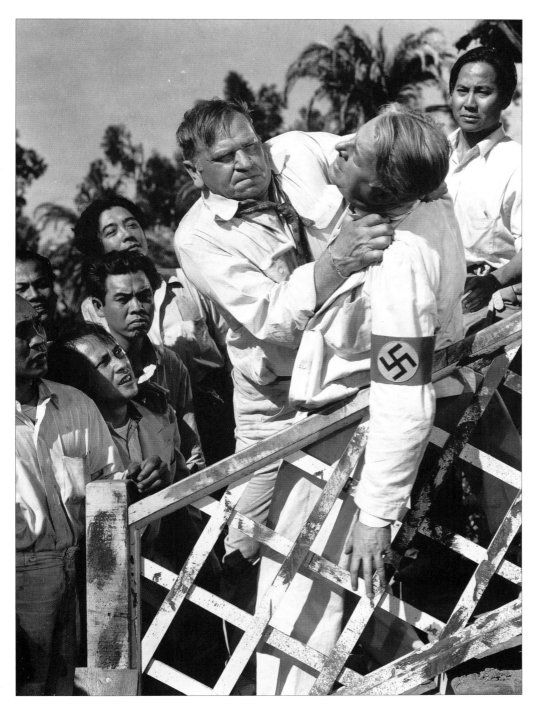

ANCHORS, BOMBS, AND MARINES AWAY

World War II was the setting for many movies celebrating the common soldier on land, sea, and air. Gregory Peck (who made the February 20, 1950, cover of *Life* magazine in his costume) got to suffer nervous collapse while driving his bird-men, stick-pushers, hell-divers, or cuck-oos—that is, his pilots (the 918th Bomb Group of the 8th Air Force)—to do the impossible (precision daylight bombing raids over Germany) in director Henry King's *Twelve O'Clock High* (1949). The first film to contain Nazi combat footage of crashing Allied planes, it also boasted an acclaimed aerial stunt in which record-holding speed pilot Paul Mantz belly-landed a 38,000-pound (17,237kg) Baker B-17 at 110 miles per hour (177kph), skidding the length of four football fields. It also boasted the role that producer Darryl Zanuck made actor Dean Jagger ditch his wig for—and for which the actor won a little bald guy.

The common water-dog, jack-tar, gob, salt, or lubber—sailor, that is—was repre-sented in numerous screen adaptations of highly imaginative, award-winning plays and prize-winning novels, from the tragic *Caine Mutiny* (1954) to the comedic *Mister Roberts* (1955). The more starkly realistic *Corvette K-225* (1943) gave an all-star treatment to both the natural hazards and the military perils of life aboard the small, mobile, convoy-protecting Canadian navy craft for which the movie was named. If you can forget about the funny hats (which were standard Royal Canadian Navy issue), the documentary style will wow you as the likes of Randolph Scott, Barry Fitzgerald, Andy Devine (away from the sad-dle), Thomas Gomez (away from the tommy gun and the tequila), and three young bucks new to the screen—Peter Lawford, Cliff Robertson, and Robert Mitchum—fight storms, submarines, Luftwaffe squadrons, and occasionally one another.

The marines had been lending their name and aid to movies portraying their macho martial tradition since *The Star-Spangled Banner* (1917). Everyone from horror star Lon Chaney—who, in *Tell It to the Marines* (1927), played one of the dramatic roles that

After fifty-two days of sequential shooting and daily editing—completed scenes could be seen three days after their takes—Wellman finished the film. He was five days ahead of schedule and again had a blockbuster on his hands. In the words of *New York Times* reviewer Bosley Crowther, the result was "the unadorned image of the misery, agony, the grief and the still irrepressible humor and dauntless mockery of the American GI."

Jarvess (John Hodiak), the company's jaded newspaperman and observer of life may have summed it up best in his variation on the chaplain's sermon:

They that wait upon the Lord shall renew their strength, shall bound up with wings as eagles...if the fog lifts. Shall run and not be weary...unless they have frozen feet. Shall walk and not faint...if they don't lose too much blood before the medics come up.

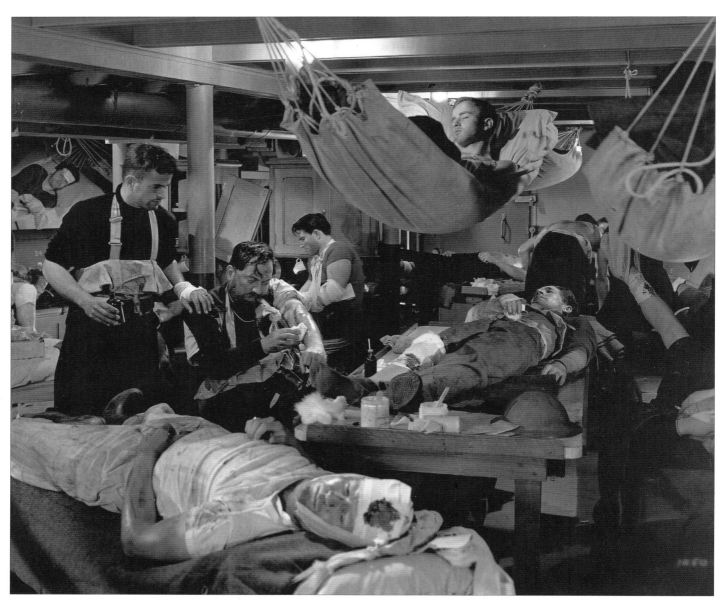

Think things are sleepy in Canada? You'll think again after watching Randolph Scott and Robert Mitchum starring in Corvette K-225 *(1943), a tribute to the Canadian navy in World War II.*

proved he didn't need monster makeup—to burly Wallace Beery (*Salute to the Marines*, 1943) to fatherly Pat O'Brien (*Marine Raiders*, 1944) had incarnated the courageous exploits of the marines. Known as devil dogs, jollies, and leathernecks, marines got their day in the klieg-light sun in such patriotic films as *Guadalcanal Diary* (1943), during which the marines (no fools) set up recruiting stations near theaters playing the film and garnered another twelve thousand new recruits.

As time went by, one actor, a national icon, came to symbolize the fighting marine: Marion Michael Morrison, or, as he was known to adoring fans the world over, John Wayne. His first and foremost marines movie was the action-packed *Sands of Iwo Jima* (1949). Inspired by the hard-won conquests of the Japanese-held islands of Iwo Jima and Tarawa, the symbolic flag-raising on Mount Suribachi, and the line "sands of Iwo Jima," which he had read in the newspaper, RKO producer Edmund Grainger cast John

Wayne as the almost mythically tough, patriarchal Sergeant Stryker (although Kirk Douglas had been the producer's first choice, Wayne had pursued the role).

Wayne was certainly tough. Even the Marine Corps technical advisers were squeamish about the Duke swiping a private across the jaw with his rifle butt during a scene showing bayonet practice. Exteriors were shot at the marine base at Camp Pendleton, California. Real Iwo Jima heroes David Shoup and Jim Crowe lent their very own wartime words to scenes of the taking of Tarawa. Captain George Schrier relived history, leading the movie patrol that raised the historic flag on film. To further ensure artistic realism, director Allan Dwan had the sculptor of the original monument, Felix W. De Weldon, flown in to position actors in the appropriate pose.

Along with *Battleground* (1949), *The Sands of Iwo Jima* (1949) kicked off a postwar cycle of films celebrating the soldiers of World War II. It also cemented Wayne's marine image. More than a decade later, during filming for *The Outsider* (1961) at Camp Pendleton, California, a group of marine recruits were asked by the director what had made them join this brutally taxing branch of the armed services. More than half of them answered, "John Wayne movies."

LET'S TEST YOUR FLIGHT FLUENCY, FLYBOY!

The following is a short glossary of World War II armed forces slang and shoptalk. See if you can match each term with its civilian translation.

TERM	TRANSLATION
1. Eggs	A: Radio antenna
2. Squadron	B: Propeller de-icer
3. Cadet widow	C: Bombs
4. Wing	D: Maneuver to cut speed before landing
5. Milk run	E: Cadet or junior pilot who hasn't flown
6. Mustard cluster	F: Parachute
7. Group	G: Copilot
8. Greenhouse	H: A mission with lots of action
9. Geese	I: An unexciting mission
10. Dodo	J: The control tower
11. Dry run	K: A flyer who is all talk
12. Chairborne troops	L: A rehearsal
13. Hangar pilot	M: Planes in formation
14. Madhouse	N: Plane engine
15. Division	O: Nonflying air force personnel
16. Junior Prom	P: The bombardier's station
17. Clothes line	Q: A girl who dates a lot of airmen
18. Overcoat	R: A poor bombing
19. Coffee grinder	S: An unlimited number of planes
20. Fishtail	T: Three or more groups of planes
21. Flight	U: Three or more squadrons
22. Bug juice	V: Two or more flights of planes
23. Stooge	W: Three or more planes

Nobody but the master, Howard Hawks, could have crafted the lingo-filled gem of wartime propaganda (and Pearl Harbor revenge flick) Air Force *(1943).*

Answers

1=C, 2=V, 3=Q, 4=T, 5=I, 6=R, 7=U, 8=P, 9=M, 10=E, 11=L, 12=O, 13=K, 14=J, 15=S, 16=H, 17=A, 18=F, 19=N, 20=D, 21=W, 22=B, 23=G.

CLEANED-UP CLASSIC

In the early 1950s, author James Jones showed that the front and P.O.W. camps weren't the only places where soldiers suffered and strived to maintain their humanity—life on an army base could be hell, too. His best-selling, 861-page novel, *From Here to Eternity*, was immensely popular and immensely graphic in its language, violence, and sexuality. This sprawling tale tells the story of the days just before the surprise attack at Pearl Harbor's Schofield Barracks, where soldiers raged against one another because they lacked an enemy to fight against.

In the novel, Sergeant Milton Warden consummates (on the beach, no less) an affair with Karen, the loose-living wife of his cowardly commanding officer, Captain Holmes. (Karen is sterile because of gonorrhea contracted during her adulteries.) Private Robert E. Lee Pruitt, a former boxer who blinded a sparring partner in his pre-army professional life, refuses to box for the army and is almost beaten to death in a regimen of persecution sanctioned by the same commanding officer. The former boxer ends up killing another soldier, anyway. Pruitt also has a relationship with Lorene, a prostitute in the base brothel. All these details made for a wonderfully entertaining and bawdy book, but they also meant that making this maelstrom into a mainstream movie would take a miracle.

The miracle took some time. Harry Cohn of Columbia Pictures bought the rights to the book (over protests from the New York office) and sent a copy to the studio's Washington representative, Raymond Bell. After Bell read the book, he said, "I feel like I spent the weekend in a whorehouse."

Over a period of almost two years, Columbia, James Jones (who was brought out to the West Coast to adapt his novel, but actually spent more of his time chasing starlets), and screenwriter Daniel Taradash labored, negotiated, rewrote, shortened, and sanitized the novel to make the script acceptable to the Breen Office (Hollywood's self-censoring organ) and the War Department.

Even with the base brothel transformed into the New Congress Club, where Pruitt's gal Lorene worked as a hostess, not a whore; even with every "f--k" deleted; even with every trace of gonorrhea obliterated (and a miscarriage added to explain Karen's sterility); even with the worst brutality taking place offscreen and restricted to one particular deviant (Ernest Borgnine as a sadistic stockade sergeant) rather than being standard army procedure; even with homosexuality deleted; even with the cuckolded and corrupt commanding officer resigning instead of being promoted by even more corrupt brass; even with the adulterous sergeant's drunk scene shortened, his lover's past affairs erased, their adultery fraught with guilt (and lines added that describe them as "scheming, sneaking and hiding"); and their lovemaking (on the sand, at least) clothed and shortened by 6 filmic feet (1.8m)...even with all this, the humanity

of these characters was irresistible to the stars who played them.

The role of Angelo Maggio, the streetwise New Yorker who takes Pruitt's side (and pays for this rebellion with his life) was juicy enough to make former Hoboken kid, songster Frank Sinatra, fly 7,000 miles (11,265km) from Africa, where he was visiting his lover, Ava Gardner, to audition for the role. For Burt Lancaster, a three-year veteran of the 5th Army, the principled but morally corrupt Sergeant Warden offered him his first chance to play a soldier. In Lorene, squeaky-clean Donna Reed saw an opportunity to break out of her prim stereotype. The role of Karen gave Deborah Kerr a chance to let her hair down (as well as have it changed from ginger to topaz blonde), strip her British accent, and strip down to a swimsuit for the first time onscreen.

Although Cohn wanted Aldo Ray to play Pruitt, the brilliant and always believable Montgomery Clift took to the gently defiant southerner with ease (with a little coaching from welterweight champ Mushy Calahan and knife-fight instructor Sergeant Sigfried Sydney). Director Fred Zinnemann claimed that Clift's talent and commitment "forced the other actors to be much better than they really were." Whether that was true or not, the performances were stellar—Lancaster, Clift, and Kerr earned Oscar nominations, Sinatra and Reed the little gold guy himself.

OPPOSITE: *Robert E. Lee Pruitt (Monty Clift, center) and his buddy Angelo Maggio (Frank Sinatra, right) indulge in a little R&R before things get ugly in* **From Here to Eternity (1953).**
ABOVE: *Soon to assume that famous prone position in the sand and foam, the adulterous Burt Lancaster and Deborah Kerr let their passion swell like the sea in* **From Here To Eternity.**

OTHER FACES, OTHER WARS

Films about average fighting men have gotten some flashy, all-star competition over the years from the disorganized misfits of *The Dirty Dozen* (1967) to the elite eighties killing machines portrayed by Sly Stallone and Chuck Norris, but dogface tributes have continued even if the soldiers aren't called dogfaces anymore.

It's amazing to think that the same director who created two of the most honored films about World War I and World War II contributed similarly to America's next armed conflict. Lewis Milestone's *Pork Chop Hill* (1959) starkly chronicled the lives of a platoon of men of the 7th Infantry's K Company as they underwent the Korean War's equivalent of Bunker Hill or Gettysburg.

In the spring of 1953, the peace talks at Panmunjom, Korea, had been dragging on for a year and a half. Both sides wanted out, but the United Nations "police action" continued because the North Koreans and Chinese communists wanted to resolve political issues before laying down their arms. Still fighting a war that

should have been over long ago, one company of weary infantrymen, a mere 70 miles (113km) from the peace conference, prepared to retake an isolated hill honeycombed with occupied bunkers before daybreak revealed them to the enemy.

K Company was told that the ridge above them would be held by the Love Company and that the barbed wire just below the bunkers would be knocked down by air strikes. They found neither to be true. American search lights mistakenly illuminated K Company to enemy fire as they struggled through the mesh. Once among the trenches, they were accidentally bombed by their own planes. And for the next two nights and three days, the bloody battle was punctuated by psychological warfare broadcast from loudspeakers along the ridge, which included constant reminders of the odds against them, pleas for peace, and even a recording of "Autumn in New York."

What kind of men could withstand this level of sacrifice? What went through their minds? What kind of man could lead them into such seeming

> **Welcome to the meat grinder.**
>
> —one of the amplified taunts that tested U.S. Army troops as they took Pork Chop Hill in the spring of 1953

Soldiers attempting to take the impossible in the Korean conflict flick **Pork Chop Hill** *(1959).*

insanity? Gregory Peck's Melville Productions decided to put it down as realistically as possible. The script, by James R. Webb, was based on retired army historian General S.L.A. Marshall's book, which in turn was derived from two hundred pages of interviews with veterans of the battle. Peck played the platoon leader, a grizzled lieutenant named Joseph P. Clemmons Jr. The real Clemmons, who had attacked the hill with 135 men and had made it to the top with only twenty-eight survivors, served as technical adviser for the project.

Milestone decided that shooting would take place in the San Fernando Valley, where he had filmed both of his earlier classics. More than five weeks of construction, 330 men, and sundry bulldozers created a 300-foot-high (91.4m) trench-filled set that led Clemmons to say, "I have to rub my eyes to realize that it's actually not Pork Chop." The cameramen had to rub their muscles after dollying the camera up and down the 700 feet (213m) of wooden track along the 33-degree slope.

The production schedule was tight—the film was shot in forty days. The style was documentary, emulating newsreel footage. The film's many night scenes were filled with shadow and fog, making them even more harrowing than they might otherwise have been. And although today the cast members (selected from 640 struggling actors) are almost all veteran screen actors, their anonymity must have added to the reality of the film.

As Private Fortsman, Harry Guardino gives one of the most compelling grieving scenes ever found in a war movie. Rip Torn is just as moving as Clemmons' brother-in-law and fellow commanding officer, Russell, the gentlemanly southern lieutenant unable to help Clemmons when his own troops are inexplicably pulled back from battle. Robert Blake plays a hapless soldier who loses his rifle and comes face-to-face with the occupants of a machine-gun nest while working as a runner between command points. And the great American actor Woody Strode gives an almost unbearably honest portrait of a soldier who faces not only his own cowardice, but also his commanding officer (Peck) in a potentially lethal showdown. One of the real Clemmons' old West Point classmates, George Shibita (the first Japanese-American to graduate from the academy), steps into the film—he plays Lieutenant O'Hashi. But the major kudos go to Peck, whose depth and determination as a good soldier in a bad place make every minute of the film ring with honesty.

You asked for misfits, marauders, and madmen? You got 'em in the immensely popular **The Dirty Dozen** *(1967).*

IN COUNTRY

We all know that Vietnam wasn't a popular war for movies until the mid-1970s. Nevertheless, by the time of the massive commitment of American troops there in 1965, there had already been a handful of films about the place GIs would come to call "in country." For years, the region had been in turmoil as a result of various communist efforts against the French rulers. These struggles and the exotic jungle locales against which they were set led to numerous films, such as *A Yank in Indo-China* (1952) and *Jump into Hell* (1955), that were little more than action flicks with a requisite amount of red-bashing

After the French defeat at Dien Bien Phu in May 1954 and Vietnam's subsequent independence, movies eulogizing the French Legionnaires and their gallant efforts began trickling out of Hollywood. Director Sam Fuller was the first filmmaker to delve into the area's complex political situation. Fuller chronicled the last days of the French in Indochina in *China Gate* (1957), which featured an array of fifties acting icons, including Gene Barry as a sergeant named Brock, Angie Dickinson as a Eurasian named Lucky Legs, future spaghetti-westerner Lee Van Cleef as Major Cham, and legendary R&B vocalist Nat King Cole as the nonsinging Goldie. In 1966 the sprawling international coproduction *Lost Command* was released, and its cast was even tonier. For this film Anthony Quinn, Alain Delon, George Segal (as an Arab), Michele Morgan, and Claudia Cardinale joined together for romance, intrigue, and antiterrorist activities.

In the end, though, the romance of the jungle faded as America waded into the only war it never won. Sixty-one years old and sporting a toupee, John Wayne glamorized U.S. involvement in his infamously gung-ho piece o' propaganda *The Green Berets*

(1968), featuring such manly (and equally venerable) men as David Jansen, Aldo Ray, Luke Askew, and Raymond St. Jacques in a strike camp named Dodge City but other filmmakers didn't see things in such Technicolor red, white, and blue.

The Boys in Company C (1978) blasted the war with both barrels as it followed a group of U.S. Marine recruits into the carnage of battle (with veteran World War II movie sergeant James Whitmore's son, James Jr., among them). *Go Tell the Spartans* (1978) showed the moral naïveté and brutal disillusionment of the first incoming troops in 1964. But even Burt Lancaster's name on the marquee couldn't make this indictment a moneymaker. *Apocalypse Now* (1979), Francis Ford Coppola's visionary adaptation of Joseph Conrad's *The Heart of Darkness*, was so big, so brilliant, and so mythical that it passed right by the American fighting man and many audiences.

Finally, in 1986 and 1987, Vietnam films came of age. Directors and writers who had seen combat in the jungles of Indochina were telling the stories that had to be told. Oliver Stone, who directed the smash-hit *Platoon* (1986), was in country by the age of twenty-one and came out fifteen months later a wounded and decorated war hero. Director Lionel Chetwync's *The Hanoi Hilton* (1987) scoped ten years of captivity for downed air force pilots, with a cast that included Michael Moriarty, Jeffrey Jones, and Paul Le Mat. *Full Metal Jacket* (1987) allowed war-film veteran and directing genius Stanley Kubrick (with the help of screenwriter and former Vietnam journalist Michael Herr) to try his hand at the psychological warfare of boot camp and the moral darkness of combat. No Vietnam movie was ever colder or bolder. And on the lighter side—considerably lighter—Robin Williams made a one-man stand against insanity as the true-to-life GI deejay Adrian Cronauer in director Barry Levinson's *Good Morning, Vietnam* (1987).

GETTING REAL

Out of all the films Vietnam has inspired, the diamond in the rough is *Hamburger Hill* (1987). Based on the now-legendary and then-Herculean effort of the 101st Airborne Division's Screaming Eagles to take hill 937 in the Ashau Valley, *Hamburger Hill* focuses on fourteen recruits in the most unblinkingly realistic and therefore most genuinely moving light imaginable. The film not only chronicles the Eagles' eleven assaults in ten days (during which 1 million pounds [453,600kg] of bombs were dropped, 152,000 [68,947kg] of which were napalm, and the casualty rate was a staggering 70 percent) in more hideous detail than most splatter movies, but also portrays the slice-of-life quiet between the firestorms.

Screenwriter James Carabatsos was the real thing (First Air Cavalry Division). He wanted to "serve" the men he had fought with in country, but it was fourteen years before he could write about his personal experiences. In the meantime, he wrote worthy scripts that somehow skirted the main issue, like the troubled returning vet film *Heroes* (1977) and Clint Eastwood's Vietnam flick, *Heartbreak Ridge* (1986).

OPPOSITE: Gene Barry tries a little tenderness with the local population in the early Vietnam love-triangle movie China Gate (1957). ABOVE: These fresh recruits may look happy now, but there won't be many of them left after walking into the world of hurt known as Hamburger Hill.

If you wanna walk out of this fuckin' place you will listen to people who know! You be an individual and I'll be taggin' your ugly, toothless face straight on its way to a long box with metal handles.

—Doc (Courtney Vance), the medic helping an F.N.G. wake up and smell the jungle java during toothbrush training in Hamburger Hill (1987)

YOU WALK THE WALK, BUT DO YOU TALK THE TALK?

This time, the GI jargon we're asking you to translate is straight from the hooches (native huts) and 11-bravos (infantry-men) of the Vietnam conflict (courtesy of the production notes for Hamburger Hill. This lingo isn't as perky as the last batch...but words change to reflect the feeling of the things they describe. It wasn't a very perky war.

TERM

1. Beaucoup dinky-dou!
2. Roundeye
3. Boom-boom
4. Victor Charley
5. F.N.G.!
6. Claymore
7. Pointman
8. Di di mow!
9. Dink
10. Chieu hoi
11. Green machine
12. Humping the boonies
13. K.I.A.
14. Cold
15. N.V.A.
16. Pig
17. Daps
18. Profile
19. Believer
20. Short time
21. Short timer
22. Deros
23. Rock 'n' roll
24. Slick
25. Mister Chuck
26. Spooky
27. Frag
28. Smoke
29. Blooper
30. Willie Peter
31. The world
32. Loach

TRANSLATION

A: Trooper with little time to serve
B: Quick sexual intercourse
C: Non-Oriental
D: Medical dispensation
E: Soldier ahead of a patrol
F: Machine gun
G: North Vietnamese army
H: The enemy
I: Killed in action
J: Being out in the field
K: U.S. Army
L: F———ing new guy
M: Derogatory slang for Viet Cong or North Vietnamese
N: Get out of here
O: Handshakes
P: Antipersonnel mine
Q: Upraised arms/invitation to surrender
R: Viet Cong
S: Sexual intercourse
T: Dead enemy
U: Very crazy
V: Any place but Vietnam
W: White phosphorous in bombs
X: Date eligible for return overseas
Y: Air strike
Z: OH-6 light observation helicopter
AA: AC-47 gunship
BB: A zone without enemy fire
CC: Troop-carrying Huey helicopter
DD: Firing on fully automatic
EE: M-79 grenade launcher
FF: To shoot a fellow U.S. soldier

When he returned from the war, Carabatsos went to Tinseltown noting "when I first came out here everyone was telling me how tough Hollywood was. I said, 'Funny, I don't see any 107s [rockets] coming in; nobody's shooting at you.' " Still, he kept getting shot down in his aspirations to create an unadorned homage to the grunt. Even after the independent producer Marcia Nasatir (*The Big Chill*, 1983), whose own son had served in Vietnam, agreed to produce Carabatsos' script, they received thirty rejections from distributors before RKO executives decided to take a chance.

British director John Irvin had spent three months in 1969 near the DMZ (demilitarized zone) making a documentary on combat photographers for the BBC. In 1981 he had directed *The Dogs of War* and signed on for *Hamburger Hill*. Irvin was the logical choice to direct. He knew from his wartime experience that "the average age of the combat soldier in Vietnam was nineteen. We're talking about kids. That was the pathos of Vietnam."

With that in mind, one thousand young unknown actors were auditioned in New York, Los Angeles, and Chicago for the roles of the fourteen recruits, all but three of whom would be dead by the film's finish.

After the roles were cast, the real work began. At the Subit Bay naval base, the actors were given squad-level training and were taught weapons familiarity by Major Albert Neal, veteran of the Korean War and of three tours in Vietnam, including the battle for Hamburger Hill. They also received three days of jungle training in preparation for their eleven-week shoot. Courtney Vance, who later won accolades for his portrayal of the tender-hearted but tormented medic, Doc, spent a week at Fort Sam Houston's Academy of Medical Science.

As crew and equipment were gathered in London, sets were constructed in the Philippines. Production designer Austin Spriggs stripped 1,800 feet (549m) of hillside of its native vegetation, replanting more than a thousand jungle trees (some of which had had the tops blasted off). An Olympic-size pool was constructed to keep thousands of pounds of mud sanitary for use during rain scenes. Special effects pyrotechnician Joe Lombardi, who had given napalm (jellied gasoline) its screen debut in *Apocalypse Now* (1979), prepared to do the same for phosphorous bombs.

Hamburger Hill is powerful drama, real (cult leader David Koresh reportedly ran the film to prepare his followers for their final stand), and visually arresting (Peter MacDonald's opening shot sweeps from a pan along Washington's Vietnam Memorial to a rushing wall of reeds with soldiers running behind it). We see both believable friendships and racial conflict between black and white troops. Soldiers grasp at escape from reality with the whores of their village (overseen by the madame known as Mama-san, played

by Vietnam's premier actress, Kieu Chink). Their already world-weary-at-twentysomething Sergeant Frantz (brought to life by Dylan McDermott) tiredly tells them before yet another assault that he won't make them "pull on the little people," but just wants them "to get their ass wet in the grass with the rest of us."

Heartbreak abounds: the whole platoon agonizingly eavesdrops on a tender, taped letter from one soldier's girlfriend, in which she tells him that her college pals call him a monster. The perpetually outraged platoon medic, Doc, appeals to his superior to make the troops wear their dog tags on their ankles as he stands over a headless casualty. And one young man just overloads on information:

> *How am I supposed to remember all this shit—panchos over your head, no half canteen...dogtags in your boots—orange pills once a week, whites daily. Don't ever walk on trails, burn the socks...the whole time I'm worried I might forget something!*

Nothing about the human heart of the dogface is forgotten here. Though overshadowed by its worthy predecessor, *Platoon* (which was made for about the same $6,500,000 price tag), *Hamburger Hill* makes up in humanity what it might lack in myth and testosterone. No toupees and swaggering here—just young men living and dying before our eyes. In the words of the 1970 poem by Major Michael Davis O'Donnell that ends the film:

> *If you are able,*
> *save for them a place*
> *inside of you*
> *and save one backward glance*
> *when you are leaving*
> *for places they can*
> *no longer go.*
> *Be not ashamed to say*
> *you loved them,*
> *though you may*
> *or may not always have.*
> *Take what they have left*
> *and what they have taught you*
> *with their dying*
> *and keep it with your own.*
> *And in that time*
> *when men decide and feel safe*
> *to call the war insane,*
> *take one moment to embrace*
> *those gentle heroes*
> *you left behind.*

May those souls rest in peace.

OPPOSITE, TOP: Charlie Sheen is all dressed up with no one to kill in Platoon *(1986). OPPOSITE, BOTTOM: Arliss Howard (left) as a grunt getting ready to walk the walk in Stanley Kubrick's sometimes surreal* Full Metal Jacket *(1987).*

Chapter Three

OLD SOLDIERS NEVER DIE

When the oldest cask is opened,
And the largest lamp is lit;...
With weeping and with laughter
Still is the story told,
How well Horatius kept the bridge
In the brave days of old.

—Lord Macaulay, *Lays of Ancient Rome* (1842)

War is the supreme test of a man in which he rises
to heights never approached in any other activity.

—General George S. Patton

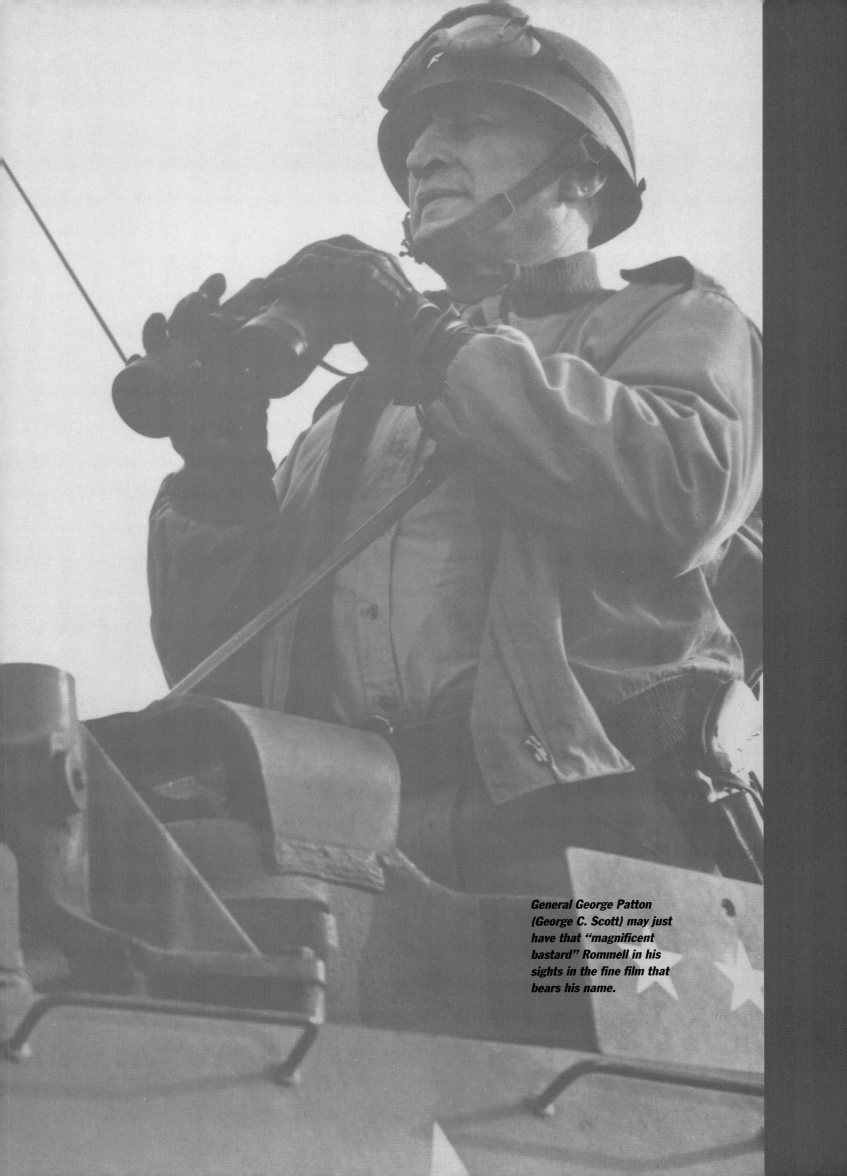

General George Patton (George C. Scott) may just have that "magnificent bastard" Rommell in his sights in the fine film that bears his name.

As flames cast flickering shadows on smoke-smudged cave walls, a group of neolithic men, women, and children huddled together, mesmerized by a lone figure striding around the fire. With his words and gestures, they could almost forget the saber-toothed cat that was outside the cave patiently waiting for them to fall asleep before slinking in to drag a screaming meal into the darkness.

The figure circling the fire was maimed and his voice was guttural, but he stood a little straighter than the rest. In one callused hand he raised a massive bone, the femur of another great cat of old. Using that bone, he had claimed the lives of three men from across the valley, as they had been drinking from his people's spring. Tomorrow he planned to take five men, armed with bones and sticks, to force this other band from their valley forever. Tonight he vowed to sit sentry by a fire of his own and use a burning branch to set the cat ablaze.

This scarred protector would be true to his harsh, heroic utterances. And by the time he died a mere fifteen years later, the whole valley would be occupied exclusively by his tribe. Every able man would have a pointed stick and shattering bone. Cats would make kills only once a fortnight. And those same smudged walls would tell of what he had done in petroglyphs of ocher as red as the blood he had spilled for his people, lifting his name and deeds into legend.

We've come a long way from cave paintings (in most cases), but a great warrior is still a glorious thing. Just ask Stormin' Norman Schwarzkopf, Colin Powell, or even Oliver North's biographers. Just ask the accountants who work for Jean Claude Van Damme, Sly Stallone, or Arnold Schwarzenegger. Just open a comic book, pick up a Tom Clancy novel, or watch a Ken Burns documentary on PBS. Peace in our time is fine, but most people believe that we need super-soldiers and military masterminds to protect us from the other ones bent on conquering the world. In the eleventh century B.C., Greek society was based on war; in the twentieth century A.D., Hollywood and numerous other entertainment centers have long been making movies based on war. As the old saying goes, art (or entertainment, anyway) does indeed imitate life.

While some great films—*The Three Musketeers* (1921), *Captain Blood* (1935), *Ben-Hur* (1959), *Star Wars* (1977), *Mad Max* (1979), and Akira Kurosawa's *Ran* (1985), for example—have exalted fictitious warriors, many of the most exciting war movies have painted cinematic portraits of real military marvels (while perhaps stretching the truth of their deeds just a bit).

BELOW: Swashbuckler Douglas Fairbanks (kneeling) as the fictional D'Artagnan in the first of many renditions of Alexandre Dumas' The Three Musketeers (1921). OPPOSITE: A face of nobility and cunning, Albert Dieudonne takes the part of Bonaparte in Abel Gance's visionary masterpiece, Napoleon (1927).

GANCE'S BIG LITTLE FRENCHMAN

One of the most momentous cinematic events of the twentieth century occurred in 1980, when Francis Ford Coppola's Zoetrope Studios presented a reconstruction of French filmmaker Abel Gance's visionary film *Napoleon* (1927). The film had been stored away in the MGM vaults since the late twenties until Zoetrope and historian Kevin Brownlow got together to recreate this historic masterpiece.

> *To make oneself understood to the people one must first speak to their eyes.*
>
> **—Napoleon Bonaparte**

Critics had rarely been more unanimous in their praise for anything except their own abilities. Judith Crist found it "the most exhilarating and satisfying cinema experience" she could remember. *New York Times* critic Vincent Canby said that "one realizes that there was once a film that justified all of the adjectives that have subsequently been debased." *Newsweek*'s Jack Kroll called it "an explosion of creativity by a man on fire." Rex Reed couldn't "imagine anything more completely enthralling or unique." New York *Daily News* reviewer Kathleen Carroll called it "a visual experience of such grandeur that it staggers the mind." *The Today Show*'s Gene Shalit claimed that it made "most of today's movies seem like insignificant pipsqueaks."

> *In war, three-quarters turns on personal character and relations; the balance of manpower and materials counts only for the remaining quarter.*
>
> **—Napoleon Bonaparte**

All this praise was for a silent movie that flopped when it was first released in 1927. It wasn't your typical silent. It ran for more than five hours (it was scaled down to 235 minutes—only about four hours—for rerelease), often on three screens simultaneously, and was planned to be only the first film of a six-part series chronicling the life of France's legendary general and emperor.

Abel Gance broke all the rules when he made *Napoleon*. To accomplish his goals, he invented enough effects to make the spectator's head spin. Rapid cross-cuts abound. Handheld shots flourish. In a sequence where a school-age Bonaparte is participating in a snowball fight, a snowball actually wallops the lens. Another kid punches the camera as if it, too, were in the fight. Gance straps it to the back of a galloping horse. He hangs it from overhead wires. He ties gyroscopes to it. He attaches it to a pendulum (which swings across a sea of faces during a tempestuous political convention in a scene that is cross-cut with shots of a real raging sea as Napoleon sails back from Corsica). And during the lusty singing of "The Marseillaise," he actually straps the camera to the chest of Russian tenor Alexander Koubitsky to help the audience experience the movement and feeling of the anthem.

Although he originally planned to use the triptych of Polyvision (simultaneous projection on three screens) in only the last two reels (chronicling Napoleon's entry into Italy), Gance liked the effect so much that he added it to two other big scenes as well. The center screen contained the "story," while the outer screens added "poetry." For battle scenes (in which Gance used as many as two thousand soldiers) and other large sequences, all the screens would join to show a huge composite picture. To film these scenes, cinematographer Jules Kruger stacked all three cameras on top of each other.

This innovation was not without personal cost. Since Gance had only one projector and no editing equipment, synchronizing his Polyvision shots required him to hold developed film up to a lighted screen, eyeballing the relationship as another reel was projected. After spending seven months at this task, his eyesight was severely damaged. Also, a piece of burning paper falling on the magnesium used for the primitive lights set seven people ablaze, blinding all of them and severely burning one of them.

Napoleon played in only eight European cities upon its release (opening night at the Paris Opera—April 7, 1927—was attended by both General Charles DeGaulle and writer and art historian André Malraux). Six months later, *The Jazz Singer* ushered in the age of talkies and pushed big, visionary, expensive silents to the margins. In despair, Gance destroyed about twenty minutes of the original triptych sequences before MGM got wind of the cinematic oddity and bought it from Gance for $450,000. MGM showed it once in its entirety in London, then took out the scissors (putting all the triptychs on a single reel so that they could be shown on one screen and filling any gaps with outtakes and discarded montages) and put the film away until 1929. When it was rereleased in its mangled, squeezed-down form, it fared even worse than it had originally.

For a while, it looked as if the conqueror were down for the count—but you can't kill greatness. The most celebrated military strategist of all time—who also initiated the study of ancient Egypt, instituted the Napoleonic Code for civil government, came

There is only one step from the sublime to the ridiculous.

—Napoleon Bonaparte

In general, my approach in Napoleon was (i) to make the spectator become an actor, (ii) to involve him at every level in the unfolding of the action, and (iii) to sweep him away on the flow of pictures.

—Abel Gance

For me, the cinema is not just pictures. It is something great, mysterious and sublime, for which one should not fail to risk one's life if the need arises.

—Abel Gance

up with the Legion of Honor, started the Bank of France enlarged the Louvre—survived a retreat from Moscow, exile on Elba, and defeat at Waterloo. He was not to be truly defeated in his lifetime or to be forgotten by history. And thanks to the efforts of such people as French filmmaker Claude Lelouch, English historian Kevin Brownlow, and American director-producer Francis Ford Coppola, Napoleon lives on in better video stores. It remains a feast to fill the belly of any film fan—and as the Little Colonel himself once said, "An army marches on its stomach."

KIRK AND KUBRICK'S THRACIAN SLAVE

Howard Fast's 1952 novel, Spartacus, had already sold more than three million copies in forty-five languages by the time Kirk Douglas' Bryna Productions and Universal Pictures decided to adapt it for the big screen. The Fast-Bryna-Universal effort is the best-known retelling of the Thracian slave-made-gladiator who led a slave revolt against the Romans in 73 B.C., amassing a force of ninety thousand people and defeating the Roman legions seven times as he swept through southern Italy, but it was not the first. Robert Montgomery Bird's The Gladiator (1831), starring Edwin Forrest, was the first play in English to be performed a thousand times during its author's lifetime.

Many of the production details for Spartacus (1960) were surprising. Although the film was set in the exotic Mediterranean, it

ABOVE: Three simultaneous screens gave viewers a world as wide as a general's arms (or ambitions) in Napoleon (1927). OPPOSITE: As Stanley Kubrick looks on, a net-and-trident-swinging Woody Strode faces off with short-sword-and-shield-slinging Kirk Douglas for gladiatorial combat with a surprising outcome in Spartacus (1960).

was shot mostly on the Universal lot or a stone's throw from Los Angeles, using old sets rebuilt for the new film. (The battle scenes were the only exception—they were shot in Spain.) Lon Chaney's and Claude Rains' old *Phantom of the Opera* (1925 and 1943, respectively) abodes became the villa of the powerful senator Gracchus (Charles Laughton). The Casbah where Charles Boyer had ambushed Hedy Lamarr in *Algiers* (1938) was downscaled to serve as a Roman slum. The French streets where Laughton had been hounded by hordes in *The Hunchback of Notre Dame* (1939) were reconstructed to become the Roman Forum. Battlefields for *All Quiet on the Western Front* (1930) and *To Hell and Back* (1955) soaked up Roman stage blood. Death Valley doubled as the Libyan gold mines from which Spartacus is plucked at the film's beginning. And William Randolph Hearst's Roman pool at San Simeon served as the setting for the homoerotic scene (cut from the original) between the hedonistic patrician leader Crassus (Laurence Olivier, whose Roman nose called for one hour and forty minutes of daily makeup) and house slave Antoninus (Tony Curtis with an accent that rings more strongly of Brooklyn than of Rome).

The script was written by novelist and screenwriter Dalton Trumbo, who had been blacklisted in the forties as one of the Hollywood Ten. In his efforts to bring the sprawling story to the screen, Trumbo crafted seven versions of the screenplay, totaling 1,534 pages.

The director was also a surprise. Stanley Kubrick, thirty-one-year-old former magazine photographer and intellectual British creator of small black-and-white films like *Fear and Desire* (1953)

and *Killer's Kiss* (1955), was not the most likely candidate to direct the most expensive film that had ever been made in Hollywood (its budget was $12 million). However, he had written and directed a cost-effective and highly successful antiwar film called *Paths of Glory* (1957) that had starred Kirk Douglas. Thanks largely to Kirk's clout, Kubrick's next venture was on the other end of the scale from cost-effective black and white. With a schedule that included fourteen months of shooting and eighteen months of editing, *Spartacus* set the standard for outstanding epics and cemented Kubrick's reputation as one of the best directors of his generation.

Of course, he did not accomplish this alone: 10,500 people put in 251,837 hours to bring the spectacle to life. Orders were put out for five thousand uniforms, 7 tons (6.3t) of costume armor, and 27 tons (24.3t) of statuary. There were so many extras for the battle scenes (including eight thousand soldiers from the Spanish army) that Kubrick had them hold numbered signs so that he could direct them from atop one of three 110-foot (33.5m) towers, where the winds whipped up to 40 miles (64.4km) per hour.

Special attention was given to the sequences that took place at the gladiatorial school of Lintus Patius. The popular Roman entertainment of pitting trained slaves, war captives, prisoners, and highly paid freemen against one another in fights to the death had begun almost two hundred years before Spartacus' time, when Marcus Brutus set three pairs of warriors against one another at his father's funeral. The blood sport caught on, and within a generation funerals for powerful men typically included dozens of such battles. Within a few more generation, hundreds of battles—some-

The Thracian slave and legendary leader Spartacus (Kirk Douglas) about to signal another of his legendary attacks against Roman forces.

times including women against dwarfs, and Christians against wild animals—were typically staged at major Roman celebrations. Once bested, the fallen fighter could ask for a decision from the crowd by raising a finger. A fluttering of handkerchiefs or a flurry of thumbs up meant life. A majority of thumbs down meant death. These bloody festivals remained popular until the fifth century.

For the film, the gladiatorial school was constructed according to two thousand-year-old designs and was filled with fascinating equipment. Vittorio Novarese, a history professor from Italy, was flown in to further ensure veracity. Each one of Hollywood's 187 stuntmen was trained for six months in gladiatorial combat, along with twenty-seven football players, including former all-American Jim Sears.

It is at the school that the "most dangerous fight in film history" takes place between Spartacus (armed with a shield and a short sword) and a towering Tunisian (Woody Strode armed with a trident and a net). This fight, which was described in only three sentences in Fast's book, required eight single-spaced pages in a shooting script, two weeks of rehearsal, and twelve days of shooting. When the Tunisian refuses to kill Spartacus at the end of the battle, he is speared by a guard while climbing to kill the ogling private audience of Romans. The spear travels along a near-invisible wire to a plate on Woody's back, where 3 inches (7.6cm) of the tip collapses, spurting glycerin and food coloring. (If a gladiator ever hesitated in the actual Roman arena, he was prodded with whips or hot irons.)

With its fine writing (weaving political intrigues, personal commitment, and a torrid yet tender love story between two ex-slaves, Spartacus and Virginia, played by a sexy Jean Simmons), superb direction (balancing intimacy with historical sweep), and great acting (which won Peter Ustinov a best supporting actor Oscar for his cunning performance as the politic slave trader, Batiatus), *Spartacus* is what you want every gladiator movie to be.

CHAPLIN OPENS HIS MOUTH

Around April 16, 1939 (his fiftieth birthday), Charles Chaplin began work on his eighty-third film—his long-awaited, first all-talking picture. Originally, he wanted a vehicle for his wife, Paulette Goddard, who had just starred in his smash hit *Modern Times* (1936). He had optioned a British best-seller called *Regency* and then had toyed with writing an exotic script set in the Orient, where Paulette would marry a White Russian. As war brewed in Germany, however, these prospects were set aside.

With the memory of the bloodshed and expense of World War I still fresh in the minds of millions, British and American policy regarding the rising German dictator, whose little mustache gave him an often-remarked resemblance to Chaplin's "Little Tramp" character, was anything but alarmist. To most of those outside his immediate sphere of control, Adolf Hitler was a power-hungry buffoon deserving only ridicule. Chaplin (who was born a scant four days before the Führer) decided to turn his talents to writing a script that would exalt a persecuted little Jewish barber and his feisty lady love, Hannah, while ridiculing the egomaniacal tyrant of Tomania, Adenoid Hynkel (also played by Chaplin, of course).

After three months of writing, Chaplin began production of his talkie debut at his studio, United Artists. The incredible expense of sound equipment had forced the improvisational actor-director to write a strict shooting script. Strictness also applied to secrecy for this anticipated movie: Chaplin closed not only the set to all outsiders, but the entire lot. He even went so far as to sue for $1 million when *Life* magazine printed a pirated still of him in Hynkel uniform.

To make his two characters as distinct from each other as possible, Chaplin filmed all the barber's sequences at the up-tempo silent standard speed of sixteen frames per second. To make Hynkel more realistic, he shot that film at twenty-five frames per second. Likewise, while the barber spoke as little as possible, Hynkel waxed loquacious with an ingenious mixture of gibberish ("I ahless un ina strutten tighten the belten") and jargonish pronouncements.

The multitalented maestro not only directed and acted, but also personally picked out material for costumes for Paulette's fry pan–swinging fräulein. He saw to the construction of a 100-foot (30.5m), 6,500-pound (2,948kg), $18,000, working cannon that was bigger than the famed 420-millimeter howitzer Big Bertha (which is riotously used in an early World War I sequence). He choreographed one of the

WHAT'S UP, DICTATOR?

Charlie Chaplin wasn't the only performer who treated Hitler with humor and ridiculed the Reich. Some of the country's most "animated" entertainers pitched in to the war effort in a way that made movie stars green with envy. Bugs at the barracks? Daffy deep behind enemy lines? Porky on the home front? These three superstars (with voices provided by the much-imitated but never equaled Mel Blanc) and many others helped boost morale, lampooned the rigors of military life, and disseminated a kinder and gentler kind of propaganda (except where German and Japanese stereotypes were concerned). Here are just a few of the standouts.

MEATLESS FRIDAY (1941)—A spider gets an object lesson in self-sacrifice when he can't devour his prey because of government meat rationing.

THE ARMY MASCOT (1942)—
Hungry hound Pluto noses his way to Camp Drafty, where he tries to horn in on the well-fed army mascot life, but ends up eating a goat's chewing tobacco.

BLITZ WOLF (1942)—"The Three Little Pigs" told propaganda-style, with two lazy isolationist pigs and a vigilant Sergeant Pork. Adolf Wolf assaults their fortress with "der mechanized huffer and puffer."

CONFUSIONS OF A NUTSY SPY (1942)—Tongue-in-cheek takeoff with Constable Porky and mongrel pooch up against railroad saboteur, the wolfish (and Aryan) Missing Lynx.

DRAFTEE DAFFY (1942)—The formerly patriotic duck (who sings "If I could be with you one hour tonight" to MacArthur's portrait) tries to buck the draft board by going to insane lengths to avoid a little old man who always says, "Well, I don't know about that."

THE DUCKTATORS (1942)—Hitler, Hirohito, and Mussolini as quacks.

JAPOTEURS (1942)—Superman vs. Japanese spies aboard the "world's largest bombing plane."

DAFFY COMMANDO (1943)—
Daffy goes behind enemy lines to bamboozle a Nazi Hawk and his bird-brained subordinate, Schultz. He gets to make hand shadows with a search light.

DER FUEHRER'S FACE (1943)—
Herr Donald Duck is a sad citizen of the Third Reich, living in a Hitler-shaped house full of Hitler-shaped things, working in a munitions factory where he spends half his time Sieg Heiling until he goes berserk and wakes from a nightmare and hugs his bedside Statue of Liberty.

PLANE DAFFY (1943)—Spy paranoia rules after a flyer (a pigeon) goes AWOL, only to end up in the clutches of the curvaceous bird Hata Mari (complete with swastika earrings). Self-professed woman-hater Daffy flies in and tries to resist her charms as she tries to get his military secrets. Jessica Rabbit, eat your heart out.

RATIONS BORED (1943)—That nutsy, violent Woody Woodpecker gets caught out of gas and without his ration book. He gets blown to kingdom come after wrangling with a gas jockey and ends up at the "Wing Rationing Board" in heaven.

SWOONER CROONER (1943)—Porky runs the Flockheed Eggcraft Factory but has a problem with his output when two crooning roosters (one a pipe-smoking replica of Bing Crosby) battle for the attentions of all the swing chicks.

YANKEE DOODLE MOUSE (1943)—Jerry goes to war with Tom dropping "hen grendades" (eggs) from a makeshift plane. Communiqués paraphrase famous wartime messages, like "SEND MORE CATS."

YOU'RE A SAP, MR. JAP (1943)—Popeye pits himself against a grotesquely stereotyped Japanese soldier. The spinach eater utters epithets about the "double-crossin' Japansies" and warns that they are saps "to make the Yankee cranky" because "Uncle Sam is gonna spanky."

FIFTH COLUMN MOUSE (1944)—A tyrannical cat (something between Sylvester and Tojo) subjugates a houseful of mice until they mobilize and declare war on him using some unique strategies.

HERR MEETS HARE (1945)—
Bugs accidentally tunnels into Germany's Black Forest (on his way to Las Vegas), only to find a rabbit-hunting Herman Göring (all rounded and pink in lederhosen) and his pet vulture. Bugs impersonates Hitler, Stalin, and a Rhinemaiden before it's all over.

Although they say that Hitler was good with the kiddies, too, Charles Chaplin's comic monster, Adenoid Hynkel, is infinitely more human in his controversial **The Great Dictator** *(1940).*

weirdest dance sequences ever devised (Hynkel's silent world-domination frolic with a huge, buoyant globe in the privacy of his office) and a more typical slapstick shave given to the strains of Brahms' *Hungarian Rhapsody* (at the end of which the barber adjusts his tie in the sheen of his client's bald pate).

As composer, Chaplin worked out an overall score on the piano as a small army of arrangers transcribed his ivory-ticklings. He edited footage of Hynkel rallies (using the double cross in place of the swastika) as direct mockery of the Sturm und Drang of famed German director Leni Riefenstahl's Nazi propaganda documentary *Triumph of the Will* (1935). He reviewed rushes daily, checking off good takes immediately and re-marking them a week to ten days later (double checks meant a keeper). He even supplied local Los Angeles orphanages with a ton of unused breakaway glass (panes of sugar) for candy.

After 170 days, 500,000 feet (152,400m) of film, and $2 million, *The Great Dictator* was "in the can." By this time, though, the winds of war had shifted and intensified. Hitler and his atrocities could no longer be overlooked.

The film ended, very deliberately, with the barber (masquerading as Hynkel) making an impassioned but decidedly pacifistic speech reminding Tomanian soldiers that "We want to live by each other's happiness, not by each other's misery." Chaplin had included a section in his opening night program entitled "Dictators Can Be Funny People." Jack Oakie, who played an Il Duce–like dictator, Benzino Napaloni of Bacteria, had publicized Chaplin's intention to give Hitler the first screening, saying:

> *And if Hitler has a sense of humor bigger than the head of a pin, he'll take one look at the picture and wonder what all the shooting is about. If he gets Charlie's point at all, he'll call his war off and retire to his mountaintop, giggling to himself.*

It all spelled less than impeccable timing for the comedian whom pundits as varied as Will Rogers and George Bernard Shaw had dubbed the only genius ever to come out of the film industry. Many critics hailed the brilliant performances while simultaneously panning its soft politics. More flak came in the form of a $645 million lawsuit (ultimately settled out of court for $90,000) over authorship of the film's concept. After the film received five Oscar nominations but no actual awards, Chaplin refused the New York Film Critic's Circle Award given to him that year. And he didn't make another film for seven years.

Ironically, Hitler may have seen his look-alike's lighthearted look at him after all. A seventeen-year-old Yugoslavian named Nikola Radosevic, who had gotten a job in Belgrade with the Nazi-controlled film selection board, claimed to have substituted Chaplin's film for another being sent to Reich troops stationed in Valjevo. After a dismayed audience reaction that included shooting at the screen (making nearby troops think a partisan attack was under way), an armored train from the Reich was sent to pick up the offending film. Years later, when Berlin fell, Soviet troops claimed to have found the same copy near Hitler's charred corpse at his Wolf's Den bunker.

LEAN'S LEGEND

They say that stark life in the desert amplifies every human quality. They also say that war brings out strange, wonderful, and terrible things in the men who excel at it. No hero was ever stranger or more amplified than Thomas Edward Lawrence. The illegitimate son of the Anglo-Irish lord Sir Thomas Robert Chapman and his family's former governess, T.E. was born in Wales in 1888 and went on to become the military legend known to the world as Lawrence of Arabia by the time he died at age forty-seven. Soldier, scholar, writer, and archaeologist, Lawrence served as an intelligence officer during World War I, advising Husayn Ibn Ali and his son Feisal in their Arab Revolt (1916) against Ottoman Turkish rule.

Lawrence's work became his passion, and it was perfect food for the press. Championing Arab solidarity (which later became a direct threat to British interests in the Middle East), he galvanized and unified warring Arab tribes in their rebellion against the Turks. A peerless guerrilla raider whose exploits could be as extravagantly heroic in saving lives as they were brutal in taking them, he led attacks on Ottoman strong points and railways, often deliberately putting his own life in jeopardy, until the Arabs finally took Damascus in 1918. Not bad for a bookworm.

A figure of mystery and romance to some Westerners, a good soldier gone native to others, and the heroic "El Aurens" to many Arabs, Lawrence was bitter to learn that the Paris Peace Conference of 1919 gave little of what he had fought so hard for to the people he had come to love and identify with. As English political leaders and a loosely joined Arab state divided power, he evaporated from the scene. He wrote of his wartime experiences in the celebrated philosophical and military text *The Seven Pillars of Wisdom*. Returning to military life under the assumed name of Shaw (to avoid being recognized), Lawrence served in the Royal Air Force (which he also wrote of in another memoir, *The Mint*) and the Tank Corps. He spent his off-hours racing boats and motorcycles.

On May 19, 1935, he died in a motorcycle accident (with only his Shaw credentials in his pocket). Some said that the accident was the suicide of a tortured homosexual. Some thought it was an assassination to prevent Lawrence from being sent to Germany to reason with Adolf Hitler. T.E. Lawrence died as much an enigma as he ever was a hero.

In 1959 director David Lean, who had already explored the enigmatic military mind-set of one heroic soldier in *The Bridge on the River Kwai* (1957), was looking for another epic to film. Although his first idea was for a project on Mahatma Gandhi, he was tempted by the beckoning figure of Lawrence. Columbia Pictures was so confident in Lean that the studio gave him carte blanche to do what he wanted—in this case, making *Lawrence of Arabia* (1962) without a budget. Robert Bolt, the esteemed English playwright who wrote *A Man for All Seasons*, was soon hard at work on a sprawling script that would bring Lawrence's exploits vividly to life.

Alec Guinness (star of *The Bridge on the River Kwai*) had recently starred as Lawrence in the West End production of a play called *Ross*, but he didn't want to play the youngish role on film. He was, however, intrigued by the benevolent but nevertheless Machiavellian King Feisal. And he was given the role—after Laurence Olivier turned it down. Marlon Brando became the next choice for Lawrence. Though enthused by the story and the prospect of working with Lean, he had a little something called *Mutiny on the Bounty* (1962) to finish filming. Albert Finney was considered for the plum role, but Lean eventually decided to give a twenty-seven-year-old unknown named Peter O'Toole the chance of a lifetime. Though he had been busy performing in Shakespeare plays in repertory at Stratford-upon-Avon—Shylock (*The Merchant of Venice*), Petruchio (*The Taming of the Shrew*), and Theisites (*Troilus and Cressida*)—O'Toole was more than willing to shave his long hair and whiskers for a London screen test and finish out the Shakespeare season in a wig and false beard. His weathered beauty, almost messianic intensity, and ability to convey a tortured emotional complexity made him perfect for the role. This Lawrence would walk the line between visionary and madman with unnerving ease.

Lean needed a cast of luminaries to surround his brightly burning new star. Though Cary Grant turned down the supporting role of General Allenby and Kirk Douglas passed on the part of the cynical American reporter Jackson Bentley, Jack Hawkins and Arthur Kennedy, respectively, were glad to accept. These actors and their fellow cast members José Ferrer (the decadent Turkish Bey), Claude Rains (the crafty old politician Dryden), Anthony Quinn (the hard-headed, mercenary Sheik Auda Abu Tayi), Anthony Quayle (the sympathetic Colonel Harry Brighton), and the star of twenty Egyptian films, Omar Sharif (the dashing and doggedly loyal Sheriff Ali ibn el Kharish), grabbed the roles without even reading the in-progress script. For them, Lean's track record was enough.

All were in for a grueling adventure. The shooting spanned ten months in Morocco, Spain, and the remote deserts of Jordan, 150 miles (241.4km) from the nearest water hole. King Hussein generously donated the services of countless camel riders, hundreds of Bedouin tribesmen, and half of the Jordanian army (some Jewish crew members had put "Protestant" on their visa applications). But he couldn't do anything about the cold desert nights, the daytime temperatures of 125°F (51.7°C) in the shade—which made many thermometers explode—and the fact that to provide each member of the 403-person cast and crew (300 of whom were Jordanians) with three months of food and water, a fully loaded 10-ton (9t) truck per person was required.

Undaunted by such obstacles, Lean was, as usual, a perfectionist on the set. For a grueling scene in which the heat-stricken character Gasim had to fall limply from his towering camel to the ground, Lean filmed twenty-five takes. Wham! Wham! Wham! When I.S. Johar, the bruised Indian actor who played Gasim, complained of aching knees, Lean asked for just one more take, then proceeded to shoot another twenty-five. Wham! Wham! Wham! Wham! Wham!

In anticipation of these rigors, O'Toole had arrived in Amman, Jordan, early to take a six-week course in the tricky art of camel riding (always sidesaddle) from Sergeant Hamdan Hamid of the Jordanian Desert Patrol. (Quinn and Guinness also insisted on going early to brush up their horsemanship.) While some of the camels, many of which had a propensity for biting, seemed to learn the word "action," not every ride was smooth. After seven months of preparation and shooting, O'Toole finally confided to one reporter on the set:

> Don't make me sound like I'm held together by safety pins, but so far I've had third-degree burns on my feet from walking in the desert, a bloody behind from learning to ride a camel, twisted ankles, pulled muscles—and two days ago I almost left my stomach on a saddle when my camel fell down and I went over the top. I'm essentially an indoor fellow. I like to go from one smoke-filled, ill-lit room to another. I haven't run as far as you just saw me run since I was fifteen.

Whatever the personal cost, all the effort produced a war-adventure masterpiece. The carefully crafted script (with scenes

Director David Lean (left) commands his forces with an authority and charisma not unlike that of his new star Peter O'Toole in the epic eyeful Lawrence of Arabia **(1962).**

of horrific warfare, tenderness, degradation, and intrigue), the vast landscapes (brilliantly caught by cameramen Freddie A. Young, Skeets Kelly, future director Nicholas Roeg, and Peter Newbrook), Maurice Jarre's hypnotic score, and the truly towering performances from every player (especially O'Toole) all garnered *Lawrence of Arabia* more than a hundred international awards. Like its subject, the film is now something of a legend. Restored, remastered, and rereleased in 1989, it is widely held to be one of the most beautiful (with the possible exception of Quinn's greenish fake nose) and complex films ever made. Ultimately it's a fine tribute to the cutthroat commander who wrote this tender epigraph "To S. A." in *The Seven Pillars of Wisdom*:

> I loved you, so I drew these tides of men into my hands
> and wrote my will across the sky in stars
> To earn your Freedom, the seven pillared worthy house,
> that your eyes might be shining for me
> When we came.

THE NINETEEN-YEAR BATTLE FOR PATTON PERFECTION

Spectacular, swaggering, pistol-packing, deeply religious and violently profane, easily moved to anger because he was first of all a fighting man, easily moved to tears because underneath all his mannered irascibility he had a kind heart, he was a strange combination of fire and ice.

—from *The New York Times* editorial obituary of General George S. Patton, published two days after his death on December 23, 1945

When the curtain rises (cinematically speaking) on Patton, we see a white-haired balding bulldog named George C. Scott, dressed in a uniform of almost Liberace-esque style, glowering in front of a five-story American flag, making the most alternately profane and tender speech ever recorded for war movies. Immediately, viewers know that something big is coming.

This juggernaut is a stunning examination of one of the few soldiers who may have been as visionary and perhaps madder than T. E. Lawrence—George S. Patton. He was the general whose Third Army moved farther and faster and had more opposition than any army in U.S. history; the tank-commanding savior of the Battle of the Bulge; the eminent military historian who had prophetic dreams and was convinced he was the reincarnation of great warriors from the past; the martinet who was relieved from leading D-Day after he slapped and humiliated a shell-shocked veteran for cowardice in a crowded hospital ward; the "pure warrior" the Nazis expected to launch the real invasion even after Allied troops had hit the beaches at Normandy; the foul-mouthed gentleman who prayed before and after every battle; the dandy who designed his own garish uniforms; the publicity hound of whom it was said "give George a headline and he's good for another 30 miles [48.3km]"; the original cold warrior who wanted to roll his tanks on to Russia after Germany surrendered; the man whom Dwight Eisenhower called "a genius in pursuit"; and one of the most respected and reviled men the military ever produced.

Patton (1970), which chronicled the glorious rise and humiliating fall of this great warrior during World War II, was nineteen years in the making and a dizzying effort. For years after Patton's death in a car accident in 1945, producer Frank McCarthy (who was also a brigadier general) had wanted to make a movie about the complex man he had known while acting as top aide to General George C. Marshall. He researched his subject using archival material, the reminiscences of military types such as generals Omar Bradley and Dwight D. Eisenhower, and Ladislas Farago's 1964 biography, *Patton: Ordeal and Triumph*.

Throughout the 1950s, however, the Pentagon refused to allow the making of a movie about the general—they were worried that a film about a powder keg like Patton could only be bad press. Patton's widow also forbade it and his son actually threatened to shoot any man who tried to make such a film.

During this period, Twentieth Century Fox and Warner Brothers took turns optioning and dropping a *Patton* project. All the while, McCarthy held to his interest. With the backing of Fox's Darryl Zanuck, he commissioned Calder Willingham to do a script, which was then reworked by Francis Ford Coppola (right out of film school). With script in hand, Zanuck recommended George C. Scott, whom he had seen as Abraham in *The Bible* (1966), for the title role (after Spencer Tracy, Burt Lancaster, Kirk Douglas, and Charlton Heston had been considered). Scott had the grit for it: when the closing-night notice had been posted for his first Broadway play, *Comes a Day*, he had punched a window and played the last act bleeding into a rubber glove before being taken to the hospital for twenty-two stitches. Zanuck felt that the tough actor was just right for the role of the World War II super-warrior.

William Wyler was wooed to direct, but he didn't like Coppola's script. McCarthy had screenwriter Jim Webb write another. With the new script, Wyler was in. Scott, however, didn't think it portrayed Patton "as multifaceted as he really was" and backed out of the role. Then the elderly Wyler learned about the location rigors and lengthy travel to Spanish locations ahead of him and resigned for health reasons.

With no director and no star, McCarthy offered the director position to Richard Brooks, John Sturges, Henry Hathaway, and Fred Zinnemann and the plum role to Robert Mitchum, Lee Marvin, Rod Steiger, and John Wayne. All declined. In the late sixties, with both the Vietnam War and its protest escalating, a film on a grand old warrior was not the best box-office bet. Finally Scott was coaxed back into the picture on the stipulation that Coppola's script would be used as a base. Franklin Schaffner, whose last project had been *Planet of the Apes* (1968), was brought in to direct. Patton's widow had died in the intervening years, his son had modified his stance, and the Pentagon had decided that even if McCarthy were going to make the movie in Spain, they had better be there to have some control.

Getting to the production stage had been dizzying, and dizzying it remained all through the process. The gruff and opinionated Scott became dedicated to ensuring an accurate portrayal—he said that he would not play the general "as a hero to please the Pentagon" or "as an obvious gung-ho bully, either." He soaked up as much information as he could, studying 3,000 feet (914.4m) of film on the general to measure the way he moved and spoke. He shaved his head daily, using a half-bald, white hairpiece to simulate Patton's aging pate. He straightened his broken beak of a nose with plastic strips and netting. He tracked down Patton's old dentist and had his own dentist make a set of Patton false teeth to extend his jawline. He added two moles, one of which was hidden on his left ear. The only thing he didn't emulate was Patton's voice, which was

> *Now I want you to remember that no dumb bastard ever won a war by dying for his country. He won it by making the other dumb bastard die for his country.*
>
> —George C. Scott as the title character in *Patton* (1970)

high and squeaky when the general got excited—"like a football coach," said Scott.

Like McCarthy and Schaffner, Scott wanted to lay all the facts out and let the audience judge for themselves. He was not a right-winger. In fact, he had gone to Vietnam and written an outraged article on American involvement for *Esquire* magazine. When later asked if he idolized the man he was playing, Scott answered:

Hell, you get paid for acting, for giving the illusion of believing, not for actually believing. For chrissakes, no, I didn't believe in what he did more than I believe in the Marquis de Sade or Frank Merriwell. This is a schizoid business to start with. The biggest mistake an actor can make is trying to resolve all the differences between himself and the character he plays.

Still, he loved Old Blood and Guts (as soldiers had nicknamed Patton) or his craft enough to insist on accuracy. When a scene regarding Patton's ruthless confrontation with General Lucien K. Truscott Jr. over an order to send men into extremely hazardous conditions during the invasion of Sicily seemed too vilifying, Scott insisted on rewriting the scene himself (with the help of Farago's book). Both director and producer approved the revision, but Fox headquarters sent it back with the order to shoot the original.

Scott literally took the refusal "lying down." In protest, he played much of the scene prone. Prickly as he was on the set, he was so utterly convincing onscreen that even some of Patton's old pals thought he was somehow more Patton than Patton. The depth and conviction of his performance became the absolute focus of the film.

Still the actor was far less than satisfied with the final product. All the fingers in the creative pie had ruined it for him. He had already snubbed Hollywood once by refusing his Oscar nomination for best supporting actor in the pool-shooting film *The Hustler* (1962). When asked about his chances for *Patton*, he said, "They won't nominate me, anyway. They're not that stupid." When the Best Actor envelope was opened and Scott's name was read, he was asleep in his bed at his house in upstate New York.

Fox had been nervous that the politicized audiences of the 1970s would see the film as hawkish. They had even deleted two late scenes from the script—one where Patton, enraged at what he finds in a liberated death camp, forces the local citizenry to clean up the carnage (the experience causes their mayor to commit suicide), and the other a final shot of Patton's grave in Luxembourg's Third Army Cemetery opening up to reveal the six thousand other graves alongside his.

It took a lot of budget muscle to recreate Montgomery's troops entering Messina for Franklin Schaffner's **Patton** *(1970)—much of the money was spent on Spain's immaculate collection of leftover Allied and Nazi tanks.*

Ironically it turned out that in that turbulent time they had nothing to worry about. McCarthy's gamble (with twenty-five "god-damns" and eighteen "sons-of-bitches" removed from the final script, according to the producer) was so honest and complete that hawks saw it as a paean to the glorious warrior, while the doves saw Patton's ultimate fall as an indictment of hawks and hubris. Was it all things to all people or just a hell of a portrait of a hell of

Old Blood and Guts (George C. Scott) takes time out for a little soul-searching before pumping back up to larger-than-life proportions in Patton (1970).

a soldier? Either way, McCarthy's tenacity and Scott's hard head, as with every truthful effort at military film biography, had done Old Blood and Guts just fine.

AND GUESS WHO I GET TO PLAY?

See if you can come up with the weekend warriors who played the real thing in these biographical films.

ROLE AND FILM	ACTOR
1. Peacemaking General Gordon in Khartoum *(1966)*	A: Laurence Olivier
2. Unstoppable Alexander the Great in Alexander *(1956)*	B: Liam Neeson
3. A paranoiac Adolf Hitler in Hitler: The Last 10 Days *(1973)*	C: Spencer Tracy
4. Manly Genghis Kahn in The Conqueror *(1955)*	D: Jeffrey Hunter
5. Dandified last-stander in Custer of the West *(1967)*	E: Charlton Heston
6. Saint Joan of Arc in Joan of Arc *(1948)*	F: Greta Garbo
7. Eyepatched Lord Horatio Nelson in That Hamilton Woman *(1941)*	G: Yul Brynner
8. Tank tactician Irwin Rommel in The Desert Fox *(1951)*	H: James Mason
9. Sharpshooter Alvin York in Sergeant York *(1941)*	I: David Niven
10. Hardy Henry II in A Lion in Winter *(1968)*	J: Omar Sharif
11. Moral Sir Thomas Moore in A Man for All Seasons *(1966)*	K: Kenneth Moore
12. Scots Robin Hood, Rob Roy, in Rob Roy *(1995)*	L: Peter O'Toole
13. Americanized archer in Robin Hood: Prince of Thieves *(1991)*	M: Robert Shaw
14. Cultivated General Robert Clive in Clive of India *(1935)*	N: Wes Studi
15. Regal Julius Caesar in Cleopatra *(1962)*	O: Rex Harrison
16. Returning General MacArthur in MacArthur *(1977)*	P: Werner Klemperer
17. Patriotic John Paul Jones in John Paul Jones *(1959)*	Q: Raymond Massey
18. WW II ace James H. Doolittle in 30 Seconds over Tokyo *(1943)*	R: Alec Guinness
19. Mexican revolutionary Emiliano Zapata in Viva Zapata *(1952)*	S: Fred MacMurray
20. WW I ace Eddie Rickenbacker in Captain Eddie *(1945)*	T: Ronald Coleman
21. Merciful Florence Nightingale in The White Angel *(1936)*	U: Herbert Lom
22. Elusive Adolf Eichmann in Operation Eichmann *(1961)*	V: Millie Perkins
23. Bullish William F. Halsey in The Gallant Hours *(1960)*	W: Richard Todd
24. Cuba's cherished Che Guevera in Che *(1969)*	X: Ingrid Bergman
25. Japanese fluent Guy Gabaldon in Hell to Eternity *(1960)*	Y: Robert Stack
26. British flyer Douglas Bader in Reach for the Sky *(1957)*	Z: Kevin Costner
27. Suicide-mission flyer Guy Gibson in Dam Busters *(1955)*	AA: James Cagney
28. Pirate Jean LaFitte in The Buccaneer *(1958)*	BB: Kay Francis
29. Suave Napoleon in War and Peace *(1956)*	CC: Richard Burton
30. Pistol-packin' Aaron Burr in Magnificent Doll *(1946)*	DD: Marlon Brando
31. Underground fighter Anne Frank in Diary of Anne Frank *(1959)*	EE: Gary Cooper
32. Secret-stealing Mata Hari in Mata Hari *(1932)*	FF: Paul Scofield
33. Abolitionist John Brown in Seven Angry Men *(1955)*	GG: Gregory Peck
34. Apache leader Geronimo in Geronimo *(1993)*	HH: John Wayne

Chapter Four

THE HOME FRONT

Keep the home fires burning.

—popular saying

Motion pictures are of the utmost importance to provide entertainment and build up the morale. Newsreels are especially of tremendous value, providing for the soldiers the means of keeping up with their friends in other theaters of war and with their families at home. The stories and the sets in the feature productions bring their home country vividly to their memories. Let's have more motion pictures.

—Lieutenant General Dwight Eisenhower while commanding the Allied Expeditionary Forces in Africa

What do you say we break a few hearts out in filmland? Frederic March and family are united in bringing you one of the best films of your lives with The Best Years of Our Lives (1946), Hollywood's most poignant portrayal of coming home from war.

Wars are not only fought on battlefields. They rage in the hearts and minds of those who never face combat. They plague the waking lives and dreams of those who have already faced it. Sacrifice is the common coin of any war, but for filmmakers World War II was unique in its screen potential. Never before had the home front been so organized and vital in its contribution to a war effort. In the United States women were "allowed" to take on defense jobs and other occupations that hitherto had been denied them, as can be seen in movies like *Swing Shift* (1984) and *A League of Their Own* (1992). Never again would Hollywood or its moviegoing public be as united in their support of a war; never again would the pain of returning veterans be as respected (and less stereotyped); and never again would the problems of returning veterans be as willingly addressed by their government and fellow citizens. World War II gave audiences a home front to be proud of, and for soldiers (who often saw films on the front or in training before the stateside public saw them) movies were a vital lifeline to all they were fighting for and hoped to return to.

BRITISH PLUCK

During World War II, "Britain can take it" was a popular refrain. And take it they did. Night after night the Blitzkrieg ("Lightning War") raged. Massive bombings, surreal barrage balloons, meticulously orchestrated blackouts, thousands of citizens sleeping in subway sta-

> *The maxim of the British people is "Business as Usual."*
>
> —Winston Churchill

tions, grim food rationing, shortages of almost every comfort, insidious V-1 and V-2 rockets, Saint Paul's Cathedral up in flames, vigilant Civil Air Wardens, the wailing sirens, the terrible waiting—it all spelled England under attack. In June 1940 the monster we've come to know as Adolf Hitler ordered an air raid on Royal Air Force and Royal Navy sites in England, marking the beginning of the Battle of Britain. On August 8 these attacks were escalated to massive daily raids over southern England. By August 24 the bombings were spread farther inland to wipe out British fighter factories. By early September London and its millions of civilians were marked as targets—and the German bombers came almost every night.

The London streets and English countryside were soon pitted with craters, strewn with rubble, and wracked with explosions, but the almost mythic English spirit proved more than a match for Hitler's arsenal. Stiff-upper-lipped, resourceful, and unruffled, Brits have wowed us in films throughout history—from David Lean and Noel Coward's coproduction of the playwright's patriotic script *In Which We Serve* (1942), which centers on the lifeboat-bound crew of a recently sunk Royal Navy destroyer as they reminisce about their lives and country, to John Boorman's richly detailed period piece *Hope and Glory* (1987), which follows a boy named Bill growing up in a London suburb during wartime.

The archetypal film portrayal of British spirit and gentility on the home front is William Wyler's wildly successful (if somewhat romanticized) *Mrs. Miniver* (1942), starring the beautiful Irish actress Greer Garson.

Mrs. Miniver began as a small series of verbal sketches written for the *London Times* by wife and mother Jan Struther. These sketches revolved around an Englishwoman's trials and tribulations at home during the war. Set in a small country village in wartime England, the film focuses on the triumphs and tragedies of an upper-class lady named Mrs. Miniver (Garson); her gentlemanly, pipe-smoking husband (Walter Pidgeon); their callow but sweet Oxfordian son, Vin (Richard Ney); their elderly aristocratic

LEFT: In **Swing Shift** *(1984), an unusually gritty Goldie Hawn learns how to get along without her man—and do a new job.*
OPPOSITE: Keeping the home fires burning isn't easy when your home is burning and you're in an air raid shelter. But Greer Garson, Walter Pidgeon, and family do a jolly good job in **Mrs. Miniver** *(1942).*

neighbor, Lady Belden (Dame Mae Witty); her headstrong grand-daughter, Carol (Teresa Wright); and various colorful people who live in the village.

Enough heartstrings are expertly plucked here for a harp solo. And despite the cast's marvelous calm in the face of war, lots of things do happen. Class prejudice is confronted in the form of Lady Belden's rose-growing competition with a common gatekeeper, Mr. Ballard, humbly portrayed by Henry Travers, better known as the angel in *It's a Wonderful Life* (1946). Vin falls in love with Carol and joins the RAF. And Mr. Miniver dashes off to Dunkirk while Mrs. Miniver confronts a downed Nazi flyer. There is death (during one of the most hair-raising car rides home ever taken by two women), decorum in the face of danger ("Fine barrage tonight, isn't it? It gets better each time"), togetherness (bedtime stories in an air raid shelter), and the destruction of one of the loveliest homes you'll ever see on film.

I never thought I could sit and read to children, say, about Cinderella, while you could hear the German planes coming. Sometimes a thousand a night came over, in waves. We had a saying [says it staccato], "I'm-gonna-getcha-I'm-gonna-getcha." That's how the planes sounded. You'd hear the bomb drop so many hundred yards that way. And you'd think, oh, that missed us. You'd think, my God, the next one's going to be a direct hit. But you'd continue to read: "and the ugly sister said," and you'd say, "Don't fidget, dear." And you'd think, My God, I can't stand it. But you bore up. And I wasn't the bravest of people, believe me.

—Jean Wood, a London resident during the Blitzkrieg, interviewed for Studs Terkel's The Good War, *an oral history of World War II*

Wyler's keen eye for spontaneous acting moments in rehearsal added to the film's considerable humanity. Loving details like a maid jauntily kicking a kitchen door closed with a swing of her heel and the stodgy Pidgeon playfully slapping his wife's derriere with a bedroom slipper help take the movie out of the fairy-tale realm. The final scene in a bombed-out church is the clincher. As the dead are mourned and villagers struggle to reassemble their lives from the rubble, the vicar (Henry Wilcoxon) gives a sermon of common cause that rouses noble sentiments in even the sturdiest cynic.

The shaft of sunlight passing shattered beams to form the shadow of a V (for victory) on the wall during the sermon was a fortunate coincidence. What was no coincidence, however, was the strength of the speech. Wyler saw to that himself—when the Japanese bombed Pearl Harbor, he rewrote the vicar's words. His rewrite was so good that both FDR and Winston Churchill had the speech printed into leaflets and dropped behind German lines. Prime Minister Churchill also wired Louis B. Mayer to praise the film as "propaganda worth 100 battleships." Nazi propaganda minister Joseph Goebbels even cited *Mrs. Miniver* as an exemplary propaganda film for the German film industry to copy.

Churchill, Roosevelt, and Goebbels weren't the film's only fans. With the United States a new member of the Allied forces, this war film exemplar hit the emotional jackpot. Audiences on both sides of the Atlantic agreed with *Time* magazine's assessment that *Mrs. Miniver* had "photographed the inner meaning instead of the outer realism of World War II." Its patriotic theme was also perfect for the first Academy Awards ceremony to be held after America's entrance into the war—*Mrs. Miniver* garnered five major awards.

The Academy Awards during the war were not unchanged that year. The statuettes were made of plaster of paris instead of gold because of the metal shortage. The 1942 ceremonies featured Jeanette MacDonald singing the national anthem and marine private Tyrone Power and air force private Alan Ladd unfurling a flag inscribed with the names of the 27,677 members of the American film industry who were serving in the armed forces. The publicists couldn't have been happier. And to top it all off, the director of *Mrs. Miniver* couldn't be present to accept his award for best direction—Colonel Wyler was on a bombing raid over Germany.

The film's publicists were less pleased about the indiscretions of the actors. During the filming, thirty-four-year-old Greer Garson had a tempestuous affair with her twenty-four-year-old screen son, the former financier Richard Ney. MGM's publicity releases unknowingly announced that "Miss Garson bought a vacation cottage at Pebble Beach" and that "Richard Ney hurried to the beach for a dip every lunch hour...even on the coldest days." It may have been their mutual love of playing the piano that drew them together. But it was only Louis B. Mayer's threats and pleading that kept their wedding engagement under wraps until the film's release. Now that's British pluck!

AMERICAN GRIT

Although Britain was hit harder than the United States, the English didn't corner the market on resolve and strength. Sure, there were enough saccharine and silly home-front scenarios floating around Tinseltown to sink a battleship. *Reveille with Beverly* (1943) put Anne Miller in the deejay's seat to serenade soulful soldiers. *Johnny Doughboy* (1943) sported the *Little Rascals'* Spanky McFarland and Alfalfa Switzer as young army camp entertainers. *Margin for Error* (1943) starred Milton Berle as a Jewish cop in charge of guarding a German consulate. *Rationing* (1944) pitted Wallace Beery against the black market of unrationed meat. *You Can't Ration Love* (1944) had coeds rationing dates because of the man shortage. *G.I. Honeymoon* (1945) made Gail Storm and Peter Cookson harassed newlyweds.... You get the picture.

Still, America played a few harp solos of her own. One of the finest was a David O. Selznick production of a project that started

TOP: Toe-tappin' Anne Miller has them standing at attention— and how—in the light and lively Reveille with Beverly *(1943)*. **ABOVE: Yes, Virginia, that is Uncle Miltie (left) keeping the home front safe from suspicious German diplomats in** Margin For Error *(1943)*. **OPPOSITE: Shirley Temple (far left), Joseph Cotten (standing at left), Jennifer Jones (standing at center), Claudette Colbert (seated at far right), and Monty Woolley (on hands and knees) pass the time with a game of Charades in the tearful** Since You Went Away *(1944)*.

in the newspapers. On June 6, 1942, Selznick had called story editor Margaret McDonnell into his office and announced that he wanted "a war story without battles." After a nine-month search in which employees at his New York, Hollywood, and London offices sifted through more than 270 possibilities, Paramount story editor William Dozier alerted the producer to Margaret Buell Wilder's column in Dayton, Ohio's *Journal Herald*, where she chronicled her wartime experiences stateside while her husband was in the service. Selznick bought the rights to the book she had compiled from her column pieces and started his own three-hundred-page screenplay elaboration: *Since You Went Away* (1944).

This movie—which had 205 speaking parts, featured 5,035 extras, took 127 days to shoot, required 15,480 feet (4,718m) of film, cost $2.78 million, and in the end ran for two hours and fifty-one minutes—follows the home-front experiences of "typical American mom" Anne Hilton (Claudette Colbert). Anne has her hands and house full. There is her college-bound daughter, Jane (Jennifer Jones, the future Mrs. Selznick); her sixteen-year-old daughter, Bridget (Shirley Temple in her first role as an adolescent); their loyal maid, Vedillia (the incomparable Hattie McDaniel); and a fussy

old boarder named Colonel Smollet (Monty Woolley sporting his famous beard). Add to the mix the Colonel's hapless young grandson, Private William Smollet (Robert Walker, who was then shakily married to his onscreen love interest, Jennifer Jones); an old family friend and old flame of Anne's, navy man Tony Willet (Joseph Cotten); and a bulldog named Soda (Dick Whittington, who appears in almost three-fourths of the picture).

It's a family affair, all right. As strong Anne pines for her absent husband, Tim (whom we never see), impressionable Jane pines for grown-up Tony and later falls for a well-meaning William, suave Tony doesn't quite let himself pine for Anne, perky Bridget (nicknamed Brig) pines for her "Pop," cowardly William pines for his grandfather's approval, and the Colonel pines for a life without a bulldog in his room, everyone somehow pulls together. Around this nucleus, life in the small town during wartime ebbs and flows. In short, Selznick creates an American microcosm that even Sherwood Anderson would have envied.

Selznick went to plenty of trouble to get it. Five separate camera crews cruised the country shooting miscellaneous home-front footage. Gossip columnist Hedda Hopper was pressed into helping

him lure Claudette Colbert into the "maternal" leading role. Memos with requests like "Please get me 500 sunsets" went out to scenic artists. The Hilton home was carefully furnished with 1,137 homey items, including Selznick's own furniture and his kids' bronzed baby shoes. Flaked gypsum and shaved ice made big snowball fights possible. To prevent the crackling rustle of dried grass, a love scene between Jones and Walker that was set in a barn had to be filmed no later than forty-eight hours after the hay bales they sat on had been cut. And the master provided rewrites, rewrites, and more rewrites.

When pressed by the *New York Herald Tribune* to confirm rumors that he gave new scenes to his cast and crew as late as the night before shooting, Selznick retorted tongue in cheek that it was sheer exaggeration: "Obviously impossible, as my associates constantly remind me. If you want to play a scene in a place like the concourse of Grand Central Terminal, or an aviation hangar, or a big modern hospital you have to give your scene designer and construction chief a little more time than that. *Since You Went Away* has scenes involving just such sets. I find that my associates always need a couple of days to construct those big production numbers. So naturally the script is always that much ahead."

Whatever Selznick dished out to the people populating his home-front world, they were up to the challenge. Though Shirley retains perhaps a tad too much of her little-girl pout, the rest of the ensemble performs faultlessly. Colbert is an especially tender rock as Mom. Her scenes of quiet agony and loneliness, often underscored by her internal monologues, are truly moving. When she reads a long-overdue letter from her husband to her two girls (both sitting at her knee), the tears start. When "Pop" is listed as MIA, get out the whole box of tissues.

As a final feat, Selznick populated his microcosm with a constellation of star cameos the likes of which Hollywood had never seen. Getting these stars was easy. The producer's last two films had been *Gone With the Wind* (1939) and *Rebecca* (1940)—it didn't hurt to do him a favor. Agnes Moorehead, prefiguring the harridan role she would one day play on the television series *Bewitched*, shines as a classic shrew named Emily Hawkins. Lionel Barrymore pops up as a clergyman. Russian star Nazimova plays a welder who works with Anne. Craig Stevens, Keenan Wynn, Andrew McGlaglen, Rhonda Fleming, Dorothy Dandridge, Ruth Roman, and many others all get little snippets of dialogue, and many make the most of them.

As for Soda (whose lack of nasal obstruction made him a snortless and castable canine), he fouled up one scene with Shirley and Monty so many times that Selznick finally crouched next to the cur and whispered, "Look, get it right this time or I promise you, that featured billing is out." Hands-on was the director's watchword here, even to the point of Selznick writing his unpublished poem *Now We Are Three* into the Hilton family scrapbook by hand. Knowing this, it's no surprise that he originally listed the screenplay credit under the names of his own kids. Papa Selznick had his heart in this one, and it shows.

HAIL THE CONQUERING HERO

> When Johnny comes marching home again, Hurrah, Hurrah!
> We'll give him a hearty welcome then, Hurrah, Hurrah!
> Oh the boys will cheer and the men will shout,
> the ladies, they will all come out,
> and we'll all be gay
> when Johnny comes marching home.
>
> —traditional song

During the hell of combat, "back home" may have seemed like a world of sure things, thick steaks, and slender sweethearts. But out of the trenches and back on the streets, those rosy visions of familiarity and comfort didn't always pan out. It was never easy picking up relationships that had been just a memory during your tour of duty and finding a way to make a living when your primary duty for the last four years had been kill or be killed. It was tough enough making the transition to peacetime if you were healthy and able-bodied. If you came back with a broken body or a broken mind, you faced a whole new kind of hell when you returned stateside.

In the early forties, Uncle Sam recognized that fact as soldiers started making their way back from the deadliest warfare ever fought. Servicing war veterans was a tradition that reached as far back as Julius Caesar and Alexander the Great. Groups like the Society of the Cincinnati (founded in 1783) had sprung up after the Civil War to aid returning fighters for the Grand Army of the Republic. World War I had inspired both the Veterans of Foreign Wars (founded in 1914) and the American Legion (founded in 1919). By the time new veterans' organizations—more than seven hundred of them—started springing up after World War II, Washington had already instituted the GI Bill of Rights by passing the Servicemen's Readjustment Act of 1944, which was designed to give veterans economic and educational assistance. But all the good intentions in the world couldn't replace an eye or a pair of legs.

Once the war was over, Hollywood's role as morale builder took a new turn. It wasn't long, however, before filmmakers and executives saw the inherent drama in the plight of disabled or disenfranchised veterans, as well as the call to honor these men. It was hoped that films that showed crippled vets winning that struggle would be an inspiration to the many other men who were walking that same road.

By 1945, the studios had swung into action. In *Pride of the Marines* (1945), Tinseltown's tender tough guy, John Garfield, tackled the real-life role of Philadelphia steelworker-turned-marine machine-gunner, Sergeant Al Schmid. This patriotic soldier had single-handedly fought off two hundred Japanese soldiers at Guadalcanal, only to be blinded when a grenade blew up in his face. Warner Brothers paid $12,000 for the film rights to Schmid's popular autobiography and crafted a picture that focused on Schmid's relationship with Ruth Hartley (Eleanor Parker), the woman he marries before shipping overseas, and how her love and loyalty helped him to accept his blindness later on. Garfield, who had spent a month living with the Schmids, turns in a powerhouse performance that he later acknowledged as the best of his career.

Sergeant Al Schmid (John Garfield) feeds the machine gun before an enemy grenade claims his eyesight in Pride of the Marines (1945).

THREE SETS OF SOULS

In 1946, with the war well over, Hollywood—in the shape of MGM's patriarchal producer, Louis B. Mayer; the Legion of Merit Medal–winning Army Air Force lieutenant colonel and renowned director, William Wyler; and three-time Pulitzer Prize–winning playwright Robert E. Sherwood (who was also a speechwriter and adviser to FDR)—offered up one of the finest war movies (if not one of the finest movies of any genre) ever made...and the battlefield was a place called H-O-M-E.

In August 1944 Mayer had been fishing around for million-dollar ideas. While browsing through national magazines, he scanned for current events that could be translated into box-office

AM I IN HEAVEN OR IS THIS JUST THE SET FOR IT?...INTRODUCING...THE HOLLYWOOD CANTEEN!!!

You've just gotten back on leave from the front lines in the Pacific. You've seen more killing than you thought you could ever cope with. A few days ago you were surrounded by the stench of bodies and the blast of bombs. Tonight you're footloose, lonely, and disoriented in Hollywood. You overheard some soldiers talking about going to some hot spot, so you followed them to 1415 Cahuenga Boulevard, one block off the Sunset Strip. Throngs of dogfaces are passing into a doorway under a sign that reads, "Through These Portals Pass the Most Beautiful Uniforms in the World."

Music pulses as you enter the building. On the makeshift stage Harry James and His Orchestra are in full swing and the Andrews Sisters are just stepping up to do a song. You reach for your wallet, hoping you have enough to cover such a swank setting, but a beautiful girl tells you there's no charge. As she takes your arm and leads you to the bar, you swear you've seen her somewhere before. When you go to pay for your coffee and sandwich, the bartender also refuses your money. You stare at his face and realize that he doesn't just look like Paul Henreid from Casablanca (1942)—he is Paul Henreid. That bald busboy dropping off dishes is Jimmy Durante. That means the girl on your arm (gulp!) is the same girl on the pinup you kept in your foxhole—it's Hedy Lamarr! Smiling broadly, she asks you to dance. You start to float. You're not dead or dreaming. You're in the Hollywood Canteen.

The Hollywood Canteen began with an actor who had been classified 4F—John Garfield had a heart murmur that kept him out of active duty. He desperately wanted to do something to help his country. So one day shortly after Pearl Harbor, he approached Bette Davis in the Warner Brothers commissary about organizing a place where GIs could actually see movie stars in person, dance with them, drink (nonalcoholic beverages) with them, be entertained by them, even be waited on by them. He had worked at the Stage Door Canteen on Broadway and wanted to contribute a thank-you along similar lines for the boys fighting Japan.

Davis loved the idea, and she quickly put her colossal clout into overdrive. With the help of forty-two Hollywood unions, she, Garfield, and an illustrious board of directors soon renovated an abandoned nightclub, making it into a swank joint that could accommodate eighteen hundred servicemen and had a special area roped off for hospital cases. She organized a continuous "who's who" of entertainment greats—often on the spur of the moment—to staff every menial

position in the club, from waiter to dishwasher. Stars and starlets served as hostesses and dance partners for the men who came—there was a strict, though sometimes broken rule that forbade them to leave with the soldiers. Some actresses would dance with hundreds of soldiers in a single night.

Where else could you cut a rug with and perhaps steal a smooch from Marlene Dietrich? Where else could you find Kay Kyser and his band every Saturday night? Where else would a blind marine be led to a private room right above the stage to listen to Eddie Cantor's jokes? Where else would Bing Crosby and his sons drop in to sing Christmas carols while Dorothy Lamour dressed up as Santa Claus? Where else could a paraplegic former soldier, after using his new prosthetic legs dancing with Deanna Durbin, say, "Gosh, if I can dance with Deanna Durbin, I can dance with the world"?

From its opening night, when civilians paid $100 a bleacher seat to watch three thousand servicemen pour in, until November 22, 1945, when it closed, the Canteen was Hollywood extravagance at its best. Among the films that memorialized its munificence, Thank Your Lucky Stars (1943) and Hollywood Canteen (1944) are the best. Sure, Joan Crawford called the latter "a very pleasant pile of shit for wartime audiences," but that may have been because every time she got surrounded by autograph hounds there, Davis would send her to the kitchen to wash dishes.

Hubba-hubba! What's that blue angel Marlene Dietrich wearing behind those feathers?

booty. He was flipping through the August issue of *Time* magazine when his attention was drawn by the picture above a five hundred-word dispatch: returning marines were leaning their weathered but beaming faces out the windows of a Pullman car, on the side of which were written two words "HOME AGAIN!"

Mayer was thunderstruck. Eureka! A movie about the trials and tribulations of a group of men from contrasting backgrounds coming home after the war to pick up the pieces of their lives. He got on the phone with skilled Americana author and screenwriter Mackinlay Kantor and proposed to pay him $12,500 for a fifty-to sixty-page treatment along those war-to-peacetime transition lines. What he got, some weeks later, was not exactly what he expected: a polished one-hundred-page blank verse manuscript comprising only the first quarter of the interweaving return stories of three American men from the same small town.

When called to the carpet, Kantor merely said that he had been in a "blank versey" frame of mine. Despite his audacity, his poem's finished length of 434 pages, and the fact that he sold it as a book called *Glory for Me* to Coward McCann publishers, Kantor was paid another $7,500 to condense it into a screenplay. He did as he was asked, but Mayer remained unsatisfied. This time, the MGM producer called Sherwood.

Mayer, Wyler, and Sherwood (who actually moved into Mayer's palatial home) secluded themselves to discuss every scene before Sherwood wrote it. As the story took shape, so did the major characters: banker Al Stevenson, former soda jerk Fred Derry, and teenager Homer Parrish. These battered souls and their families would be the film's focus. With three interweaving stories to shoot, this was going to be a big

film, and Wyler wanted a production staff that was up to the challenge. Gregg Toland, director of photography on such legendary films as *Citizen Kane* (1941), was hired to lens the picture and give it the almost documentary depth of focus he was famous for.

To get to this realism, Toland insisted that none of the male characters wear movie makeup and that Broadway costume designer Irene Sharaff dress the cast-to-be in clothing completely devoid of color to make his black-and-white photography that much more lucid. New York set designer George Jenkins imposed his own demands. Asked to create forty-five complete working sets—most major feature films required only a handful of smaller sets—he insisted that room dimensions be kept to reality, not built overly large to accommodate both actors and crew. This necessitated roll-away walls on almost every set and a constant juggling act with crew and cameras.

Casting was just as exacting. Al the banker would be played by Fredric March, who had studied finance at the University of Wisconsin and had worked at the National City Bank of New York until a recovery from appendicitis gave him time to rethink his career choice. Fred Derry would be given life by former accountant and third son of a Southern Baptist minister, Dana Andrews. Al's daughter, Peggy (who falls in love with the married Fred), would be portrayed by Theresa Wright, who had hoofed it to Hollywood with the New York cast of the play *Life with Father*.

Virginia Mayo shed her good-girl image to play Fred's gold-digging glamour-girl of a wife, Marie. Composer, songster, and pianist Hoagy Carmichael, who had made such a hit in films like *To Have and Have Not* (1943), scored as the composed bar proprietor, Butch. Myrna Loy, who had been relegated to playing Oriental vamps for twelve years—until Rudolf Valentino plucked her from oblivion in a dance line —snagged the role of Al's refined and resigned wife, Milly. Oklahoma-born Cathy O'Donnell, who played Homer's long-suffering sweetheart, was discovered in a drugstore.

Then there was Homer. In Sherwood's original script he was a shell-shocked and spastic sailor. However, when Mayer and Wyler saw a Marine Signal Corps training film called *The Diary of a Sergeant*, all that changed.

The film's star, Harold Russell, a husky young supermarket manager from Cambridge, Massachusetts, had enlisted two months after Pearl Harbor. On D-Day he was working as a demolitions instructor at Camp Mackal when half a pound (226.8 g) of TNT blew up in his grasp. He woke up without hands. His aptitude with

> Now is when I know I'm helpless. My hands are down there on the bed. I can't put them on again without calling to somebody. I can't smoke a cigarette. I can't read a book. If the door should blow shut I can't open it to get out of this room. I'm as dependent as a baby that can't get anything except to cry for it. Well, now you know, Wilma. Now you have an idea of what it is. I guess you don't know what to say.
>
> —real WWII veteran Harold Russell as the handless Homer Parrish in *The Best Years of Our Lives* (1946)

Fred Derry (Dana Andrews, center) gives Homer Parrish (real-life amputee Harold Russell, left) a little brotherly backup at the home front in William Wyler's towering The Best Years of Our Lives (1946).

(and attitude about) the prosthetic clamping hooks that were sup-plied to him was so miraculous that he was made a celluloid mod-el for other amputees to learn from. After interviewing Russell at length, Sherwood put much of the boy's own history into the script.

And what a script it was. What a movie it is. The characters and the stress of the postwar situations they find themselves in feel as familiar as if they were family (even fifty years later). Most of the illus-trious cast members give the performances of their careers. March is a weary wonder as the well-intentioned banker with a drinking prob-lem who must wrangle with his tight-fisted company's policy on giv-ing loans to veterans. Andrews' noble loser, who soars in the air force only to hit a career brick wall on the home front, is courageously underplayed. Loy is low-key yet alluring (she and March have some incredibly frank and sexy scenes). Wright is just real. But the unac-torly Harold Russell is king of this fine ensemble. Glamorous? Hardly. Attractive? Not really. Yet he has the stuff of genuine heroism—the quiet strength, the humility, the ease. Wyler also makes plenty of use of his hook expertise and everyone else's discomfort with it.

The Best Years of Our Lives swept the 1946 Oscars. Harold Russell picked up two gold statuettes: one for best supporting actor (though Andrews deserved it as well) and another for bringing hope and courage to his fellow veterans. Like Homer, Harold mar-ried his childhood sweetheart. After writing an autobiography, *Victory in My Hands* (1949), he became the national commander of AMVETS and a leader in the World Veteran Federation. Like the work he continued, this film lives on.

DOING IT THE HARD WAY

John Garfield may have stuck his cane in the door for films deal-ing with the realities of men returning home from war less than whole. Harold Russell may have pried the door open a bit wider with his dexterous hooks and his honest portrayal. But another twenty-year-old movie-acting novice (though no acting novice by any means) rammed the doors off their hinges with his wheelchair in an uncompromising film that would launch him on the way to becoming the greatest American actor of his generation. The actor is Marlon Brando; the movie is *The Men* (1950).

The film's producer, Stanley Kramer, had already established a reputation as a behind-the-camera force with grit and integrity. With writer Carl Foreman he had crafted *Champion* (1949), the first film to depict the brutalities of boxing, and *Home of the Brave* (1949), which ripped the lid off racism in the military. He went on to produce such classics of conscience as *High Noon* (1952), *The Member of the Wedding* (1952), *The Caine Mutiny* (1954), *On the Beach* (1959), *Inherit the Wind* (1960), *Judgment at Nuremberg* (1961), and *Guess Who's Coming to Dinner* (1967), but in 1950 he was look-

Myrna Loy (left), Fredric March, and Theresa Wright, as a family in trouble, give the best performances of their lives in **The Best Years of Our Lives** *(1946).*

ing for an unflinching examination of the war's many veterans who were fighting to fit back into society.

Inspired by Kramer's idea, Foreman spent several months in Van Nuys' California Veterans Hospital getting to know the men there and the chief surgeon on the paraplegic ward, Dr. Ernest Bors, who had helped so many of them through the hell of readjustment. The story Foreman created following his visit was a composite of the experiences of many of the veterans he had met (forty-five of them would play small roles in the film). It centered on the struggles of Ken Wilczech, an army lieutenant inspired by Ted Anderson, a hospital resident (who ended up serving as a technical adviser) who had been paralyzed in Dorscheid, Germany, on the cold morning of March 26, 1945, when he was shot in the neck by a sniper.

Ken's inner turmoil and battle with the world around him would need the spark of an exceptional actor. Marlon Brando, who had already carved a name for himself as the volatile, Stella-screaming Stanley Kowalski in the Broadway run of Tennessee Williams' *A Streetcar Named Desire*, had been wooed by Hollywood ever since he took New York by storm, but had turned down role after role, citing what he considered empty material and the confinement of a contract to a major studio. Kramer offered him the sensitive role of Ken in *The Men* with no strings attached—and to Kramer's surprise, Brando accepted.

The surprises weren't over. The headstrong method actor was no sooner in Hollywood than he shunned celebrity society to live with his aunt and grandmother in a modest house while he studied Charlie Chaplin and John Barrymore films for acting technique. Next, he arranged to check himself into the Veterans Hospital's thirty-two-bed paraplegic ward for a four-week stay. The men there had no patience for a "toothpaste smile," but Brando wasn't a Hollywood hunk going through the motions for a publicity gimmick; he was there to work. He refused to use his legs and, like every paraplegic, learned to haul himself around the ward using his upper body strength alone.

Brando dived in, joining the vets in their grueling regimen of physical rehabilitation (including rope climbing with just his arms). He also tried to keep up with them outside—in his wheelchair. Off the grounds he drank with them at their local hangout, the Pump Room (where he once hoisted himself out of his chair and began tap dancing in testament to the healing powers of faith to shut up a proselytizing, sacrifice-spouting, able-bodied drunk). He learned how to use a manually controlled Oldsmobile (when his car stalled and he broke his training to get out to push it, his legs were so weak that he fell on his face) and even showed up for Hollywood story conferences in his wheelchair.

Even though he got adept enough in his role that he was named an honorable paraplegic by his buddies and even fooled a hospital therapist (who referred to him as "D-10"—paralyzed from the tenth dorsal vertebra down), the maestro had his slips. He had to remind himself constantly that his balance would be affected by the loss of feeling in his legs (real paraplegics often had to lean back for stability). Also, he admitted, he would occasionally "forget and lean down and scratch my ankle."

The result of all this preparation (plus two additional weeks of rehearsal with the entire cast in the hospital) is a picture that pulls nary a punch. Not only is the tormented Brando completely convincing through his struggle to reintegrate with society, but all the players give performances straight from the heart in scene after scene.

One actor who needed no research was Arthur Jurado, a Mexican-American veteran who scored the role of Ken's only upbeat friend, Angel. The workout scenes where he spurs Brando to surmount his disability smack of real camaraderie and the handsome Jurado seems strangely...Brandoesque. In fact, he paid such close attention to his scene partner's technique that Brando later admitted, "I'm glad the picture is almost over because this guy is stealing all my thunder." The compliment is justified, for Angel's ultimate fate, and its effect on Brando, makes for the movie's most moving moment.

Though grim by any standard—it was banned in England for its frank talk (for 1950) about sex—*The Men* gave movie audiences everywhere a taste of postwar emotional reality and an introduction to the actor who would come to embody this new reality. As for Brando, did his triumph lead to poolside complacency and new scripts flooding in? Hardly. He took the profits from his salary, which his father had invested in sixteen hundred head of Nebraska cattle, and used them to study art, literature, and psychology at New York's New School of Social Research.

The hero is not fed on sweets.
Daily his own heart he eats.

—**Ralph Waldo Emerson**

*Established star Theresa Wright fought for the role of the fiancée who must fight her way back into the heart of her estranged soldier (Marlon Brando) in Fred Zinneman's **The Men** (1950).*

WHAT DID YOU DO IN THE WAR, DADDY?

To my mind, few if any of the other agencies of public appeal and influence have done more than the motion picture industry in consolidating the will of the people to meet the war emergency and contribute to the victory of the United Nations.

—First Lady of China Madame Chiang Kai-Shek

By 1943 the motion picture industry alone had 36,500 men and women in the armed forces. Within the massive contribution that the entire Hollywood firmament made to the whole war effort, individual stars played wildly varying roles. And there were lots of avenues for their talents. For instance, The Signal Corps (Hollywood's film-producing alliance with the government) made scores of propaganda and training films (on topics ranging from sexual hygiene to ski mountaineering to battle formations to the uses of manila rope). The Hollywood Victory Committee (formed three days after the attack on Pearl Harbor) harnessed star power to entertain members of the armed services. The USO (United Service Organization) took entertainment to stateside camps and the foxhole circuit (where 6,810 artists logged 5,237,000 miles [8,427,904km] between December 7, 1941, and September 8, 1945). War Bond drives had stars touring the country raising millions of defense dollars. There were blood donor campaigns, hospital visits, copper salvage drives, and buy-a-bomber campaigns. The Hollywood Canteen gave GIs in Los Angeles a home away from home where they could hobnob with the stars. Some stars even saw real combat. See if you can match the screen personalities with some of their wartime stunts and stints.

STAR	SERVICE
1. Katharine Hepburn	A: This carrot top covered 200,000 miles (321,860km) in four years with the USO and got his biggest laughs when he orchestrated a cupid in a nearby fountain to stop peeing during his harp solo.
2. James Stewart	B: This amateur magician entertained the troops with the thirty-minute "Wonder Show," in which he might hypnotize a chicken or saw Marlene Dietrich in half.
3. Buster Keaton	C: This conscientious objector almost wrote his own epitaph when he said, "I'll praise the Lord but I won't pass the ammunition." However, his work as a medical corpsman and the donation of his salary to the Red Cross turned him from a heel to a hero.
4. Edgar Bergen	D: This forty-three-year-old tough guy had already served on the USS Leviathan in WWI. While he toured with the USO, paratroopers taught him how to jump. Leaping from a bar one night yelling, "Geronimo!" he knocked himself out on the floor.
5. Douglas Fairbanks, Jr.	E: Even with a bad shoulder, this thirty-five-year-old celluloid warrior flew to Washington, D.C., to beg his buddy John Ford to find him a spot in the navy. To his perpetual shame, he was never admitted into the armed services.
6. Wayne Morris	F: This fifty-year-old coin flipper refereed boxing matches for "The Cavalcade of Sports" at army and navy bases.
7. John Wayne	G: Lionel Barrymore convinced this forty-one-year-old WWI vet that people would pay good money to hear him sing badly, so he graced the USO with "Pistol Packin' Mama."
8. Orson Welles	H: This heartthrob was rumored to have worked for British intelligence, but changed his citizenship to U.S. so that his heiress wife, Barbara Hutton, could get her money out of frozen British banks and contribute to wartime charities.
9. Lew Ayers	I: This star had her home searched by the FBI for arms because she and her sister, Olivia, were born in Tokyo.
10. Marlene Dietrich	J: This starlet snipped off her trademark peekaboo bangs when it was learned that as many as twenty thousand women working in defense plants were wearing the same do and getting it caught in machinery.

11. Betty Grable

12. Groucho Marx

13. Charles Laughton

14. Clark Gable

15. Henry Fonda

16. Bette Davis

17. James Cagney

18. Carole Lombard

19. Edward G. Robinson

20. Joan Fontaine

21. Joan Crawford

22. Cary Grant

23. Lucille Ball

24. Paulette Goddard

25. Myrna Loy

26. Lana Turner

27. Hedy Lamarr

28. Abbott and Costello

K: It was no joke when this "lovable" comedienne heard noises in a new filling while coming home from the dentist. When she alerted the FBI, they found a transmitter in the area belonging to a gardener who was part of a Japanese spy ring.

L: It was even less of a joke when this beloved comedienne kicked off the first big War Bond tour in her home state of Indiana, sold $2 million worth in one day, and then perished when her plane crashed into Olcott Mountain, 35 miles (56.3km) west of Las Vegas.

M: This activist actress narrated a short film called Women in Defense, written by Eleanor Roosevelt.

N: This clown, along with Rudy Vallee, Caesar Romero, Robert Young, and Victor Borge, was a member of the California Evacuation Corps, ambulance drivers who knew the shortcuts to local hospitals in case of Japanese bombing. Most members also owned station wagons.

O: On one hospital visit, this entertainer and his dummy threw voice into a shell-shocked soldier who hadn't said a word in eight days.

P: This star of I Wanted Wings (1941) got his wings in Naval Aviation and took part in raids on Wake Island, Iwo Jima, and Okinawa. Three of his bullet-riddled planes had to be scrapped during his fifty-seven missions, during which he downed seven enemy planes and helped sink a submarine, a gunboat, and two destroyers. He received four Distinguished Flying Crosses and two Air Medals.

Q: These clowns did a command performance of "Who's on First" at the White House, where one of them kept referring to Roosevelt as "the prez."

R: This schnozzola offered his and Marlene Dietrich's domestic services to the highest bidder. Together they ended up spending days washing apartment windows.

S: This flawlessly beautiful star who had once been stricken with facial boils, as the result of a sulfa drug for the flu, had a special ease with facially maimed soldiers in hospitals, one of whom she had a tender affair with while her own husband was being knighted by the Queen of England.

T: This son of a swashbuckler swashed a little himself as he led navy commando raids on Mediterranean islands to win a Silver Star, the Italian War Cross, and the French Legion of Honor's Croix de Guerre.

U: This star of They Were Expendable (1945) got experience commanding PT boats in the Panama Canal and South Pacific, participated in the Normandy invasion, lost 22 pounds (10kg) from malaria, and received the Bronze Star.

V: This diva offered to take Carole Lombard's role in They All Kissed the Bride (1942) and donate her salary to charity. When her agent demanded his cut, she fired him.

W: This quiet American star left a cushy job as a flight instructor and became a meticulous bomber captain of twenty combat missions, earning him an Air Medal, an Oak Leaf Cluster, and a Distinguished Flying Cross.

X: This blonde bombshell, who had grown up in a war-torn Europe, learned how to handle a crowd from Danny Thomas and proceeded to entertain more troops on "The Fox Hole Circuit" (sometimes playing a musical saw between her legs), kiss more soldiers for free, sell more kisses stateside, sing "Lili Marlene" to more German POWs, and sleep with more generals (including Patton) than any other entertainer during the war.

Y: This little Caesar actually pulled a "Chicago typewriter" from a violin case to entertain the troops.

Z: This much-publicized model American soldier never went to war, but kept his film output to no more than four films a year to keep from being boosted into a higher tax bracket.

AA: This hunk hunkered down at a Lockheed plant, making bombers before becoming a movie star.

29. Frank Sinatra

30. Robert Montgomery

31. Sterling Hayden

32. Spencer Tracy

33. George Raft

34. Gary Cooper

35. Jimmy Durante

36. Merle Oberon

37. Humphrey Bogart

38. Gregory Peck

39. Robert Mitchum

40. Ronald Reagan

41. Harpo Marx

42. Veronica Lake

43. Jack Benny

44. Lena Horne

BB: *After giving up Hollywood stardom to fight for England and break his legs training as a British commando, this renegade changed his name to John Hamilton for the duration (so as not to get the star treatment), enlisted in marine boot camp at Paris Island, went to Officer Candidate School at Quantico, joined the Office of Strategic Services, fought under the communist Yugoslavian guerrilla leader Tito, ran supplies to partisans, received the Silver Star, and spy-photographed fifty-three ports from Germany to Norway.*

CC: *A photograph of this pin-up queen (wearing nothing but an officer's jacket) was laid under a grid and used to instruct soldiers in map reading. She also planted lipstick marks on GIs' casts.*

DD: *This notorious tightwad donated his beloved Maxwell car on the radio for scrap to build bombers. Sound effects had a later bomber sputtering and grinding.*

EE: *This left-leaning leading lady sang the following as she knitted for soldiers: "Hitler has only one ball, Göring has two but they are small, Himmler has something similar but Goebbels has no balls at all."*

FF: *This sweater girl sold kisses for $50,000 worth of war bonds per pucker.*

GG: *This feisty proprietress of the Hollywood Canteen told a group of factory workers in Oklahoma City that they had better work at top level or they would not be her idea of Americans. Hardline as she was, she sold autographs and photos for war bonds and made $2 million in two days.*

HH: *This acting legend sold $500,000 worth of war bonds on Wall Street by reading from the Bill of Rights.*

II: *After doing a mock strip tease in a war bond rally at Madison Square Garden, this siren sold her hat for $30,000 and her elbowless crimson gloves for $25,000.*

JJ: *With his wife's untimely death, this forty-one-year-old enlisted in the air force, shaving his trademark mustache for anonymity and telling friends that "I don't expect to come back and don't give a hoot." He did come back, but not until he had made a training film about the dangerous occupation of aerial gunners, took too many chances, flew too many missions, and stimulated Hermann Göring to offer any German pilot a promotion, a leave, and a cash reward for capturing him and bringing him back to the base for dinner.*

KK: *This taciturn, thirty-seven-year-old leading man enlisted in the navy without telling his studio and taught his daughter Jane's prep-school version of "Anchors Aweigh" to other officers. He became a specialist at submarine detection and received the Bronze Star and a presidential citation.*

LL: *When he tried to join a war bond caravan without his greasepaint mustache, this funny man was stopped by a cop, who, when told who he was, replied, "Sure, and I'm Jimmy Durante."*

MM: *This siren's "Hedy" kisses sold $17 million worth of war bonds in one day.*

NN: *When this crooner saw that black GIs had been placed in the back of a USO crowd, she left the stage and sang from the back.*

OO: *When this forty-three-year-old hoofer was heckled as being out of shape during his USO rendition of "I'm a Yankee Doodle Dandy," he politely asked the soldier to accompany him on stage and hop from foot to foot as the maestro sang and danced. The soldier collapsed after two choruses.*

PP: *This crooner's punctured eardrum kept him civilian, much to the anger of many a dogface. But he did sell songs to the highest bidder at war bond rallies.*

QQ: *This leading man was classified 4-F because of a ruptured disc he received from Martha Graham during a dance class.*

RR: *An improperly set broken hip kept this strong, silent type out of battle, but he finally opened his mouth for the USO with Lou Gehrig's famous farewell speech.*

OTHER HOMES, OTHER FRONTS

During the mid-forties, most of the world was at war, with combat and occupation tearing apart millions of homes and families. Many nations—including Russia, Germany, Japan, and France—made substantial contributions to film from the years just prior to World War II to those just after it. But one country—physically ravaged by fighting and torn

Future Italian efforts would continue to reexamine the divided loyalties and destruction particular to that country during the war. Bernardo Bertolucci's *The Conformist* (1970) exposed the seedy lure of fascism for the Italian upper classes. In 1976 he spent five hours exploring the entire Italian class system and its evolution through the war in the star-studded *1900* (whose cast included Robert De Niro, Burt Lancaster, Gerard Depardieu, Dominique Sanda, Donald Suth- erland, and Sterling Hayden).

Lina Wertmuller depicted the possibility of a petty crook (Giancarlo Giannini) bringing some semblance of humanity into a Nazi concentration camp in *Seven Beauties* (1976). The Tavani brothers' *Night of the Shooting Stars* (1982) drew sides with its battle between partisans and fascists in a field of towering wheat. Ettore Scoia scored with the Academy Award–winning *A Special Day* (1977), which brought a pair of unlikely lonely hearts together on a day when most of Rome has gone elsewhere to hear Il Duce (Mussolini) speak. Marcello Mastroianni as an aging homosexual and Sophia Loren as a neglected housewife are a mismatch made in heaven.

TOP: Rinaldo Smerdoni and Franco Interlenghi's enterprise during the Nazi occupation of Italy is about to land them in jail in Vittorio De Sica's The Bicycle Thief *(1948)*. BOTTOM: Italian orphan Alfonsino Pasca (right) has his eye on both Dots M. Johnson's heart and wallet in Paisan *(1946)*, written by Federico Fellini and directed by Roberto Rosselini.

between the support of a fascist dictator and Allied liberators—gave birth to a whole new film movement. Italian Neorealism got its start from home-front filmmakers like Roberto Rossellini and Vittorio De Sica.

Conceived during fascist rule, Rossellini's *Rome, Open City* (1945) harnessed the earthy talents of Anna Magnani to illustrate the horrors of occupation. His *Paisan* (1946) detailed six separate encounters between American soldiers and the Italians they were liberating; one segment focused on the friendship between a black American GI (Dots M. Johnson) and the little Neapolitan waif (Alfonsino Pasca) who simultaneously befriends him and plans to rob him. His *Germany, Year Zero* (1947) zeroed in on the devastating psychological and moral toll the war took on residents of Berlin.

De Sica, whose classic *The Bicycle Thief* (1948) portrayed the poverty and desperation of postwar Italy, had scored earlier with *Shoeshine* (1946), a wartime story of two destitute boys who run errands for GIs, only to end up fighting the horrors of reformatory life.

MADONNA
AND
CHILD

Sophia Loren—who had grown up during the war in Italy, had gone on to win a Naples beauty contest (where her prize was free wallpaper for her family's parlor, two 8- by 10-inch [20.3 x 25.4cm] pictures of herself, and $40 in lire), and had graduated to play comediennes and sexpots in paltry pictures that took advantage of her most obvious assets—was elevated overnight to recognition as an accomplished actress in *Two Women* (1961), De Sica's wrenching story of mother and daughter caught in the middle of the war's fury.

Oddly enough, Sophia was first cast as the daughter of the duo, with George Cukor set to direct and Anna Magnani to play mama. But Magnani thought the statuesque Loren too tall and too old to play her offspring and rejected the part. The script was rewritten and the age of Rosetta, the daughter, was reduced to thirteen. With this alteration Sophia was up for the role of the long-suffering, maternal Cesira. Cukor, meanwhile had abandoned ship to film *Let's Make Love* (1961) with the other sex symbol of the decade, Marilyn Monroe, and De Sica had taken the directoral reins.

When Loren balked at going so far against type, De Sica told her, "If you become this woman without any thought as to how you look, without trying to strain your emotions, letting everything flow into this character, I guarantee you, you will have the role of your life." He was right. When the widowed grocer and her daughter (Eleanora Brown) flee the squalor of 1943 Rome (and the amorous embraces of a coal merchant played by the studly Raf Vallone) for the rural poverty and safety of Cesira's southern ancestral village of Saint Eufemia, they hop right out of the frying pan and into the fiery chaos of Italy at the end of the war. Stalled trains, bullying blackshirts, English soldiers seeking refuge, Russian deserters, strafing German planes, fleeing Nazis, arriving Americans, hardship, and starvation all await the two women.

Embodying cynical strength that covers a kind heart and maternal ferocity, Loren charms not only the audience, but also a political intellectual named Michele (an against-type Jean-Paul Belmondo). Sadly, it isn't long before war tears that bond asunder and delivers Cesira the most savage blow of all in the refuge of an abandoned church: she and her daughter are raped by Moroccan soldiers. The emotional power of Loren's performance, which is like a force of nature, won her more than ten international film awards, including the Cannes Film Festival best actress prize, the British Oscar, and the New York Film Critics Award.

Sex symbols don't cry, but great actresses do. A mother's anguish wracks the face of Sophia Loren in what may be her all-time greatest role—Cesira in De Sica's unforgettable Two Women *(1961).*

THE LITTLEST CASUALTY

After the horror of the Third Reich, prosecuting Nazis became the popular focus of many World War II films. There were the real-life Nuremberg war-crime trials, as depicted in Stanley Kramer's star-studded *Judgment at Nuremberg* (1961), which featured Montgomery Clift at the ragged end of his brilliant film career as well as a stellar study in understatement by Burt Lancaster as a Nazi with a conscience.

There have been marginally plausible thrillers such as the Nazi–serial killer whodunit *The Night of the Generals* (1966), with Peter O'Toole and Omar Sharif paired up a little less romantically than they had been in *Lawrence of Arabia* (1962). There were even totally fanciful ones like Nazi dentistry at its best in *Marathon Man* (1976), in which Laurence Olivier plays a white-haired, fish-eyed, quintessentially cold-blooded killer, or a genetic nightmare at its worst in *The Boys from Brazil* (1978), in which Olivier plays a Jewish Nazi hunter à la Simon Wiesenthal. Rarely, however, has the focus shifted away from the glamorous villains to take in the toll on the victims of the Holocaust, let alone its smallest survivors. That welcome exception is director Fred Zinnemann's *The Search* (1948), a story of small-scale postwar pathos.

Filmed amid the rubble of a bombed-out Germany, *The Search* is about the plight of children. It follows the lives of three characters in postwar Europe: a soon-to-depart American soldier named Ralph Stevenson (Montgomery Clift in his first screen role); an adorable Hungarian amnesiac survivor of Auschwitz, the ten-year-old Karel (Ivan Jandl); and the boy's mother (Jarmila Novotna), who is thought to be dead but is in reality desperately searching for her son.

Ralph finds the starving Karel scavenging in the rubble after the boy has fled a children's refugee camp. Not knowing what to do, the soldier grudgingly takes the tyke under his wing and, after earning his trust, involuntarily begins to develop a bond with him (as does everyone in the audience). As Karel learns English and the fragments of his past come slowly back to him, so does the world of pain he endured after losing his mother. Ralph is convinced that she is dead and plans to bring Karel to the United States later, as soon as he can get a job. But the boy, believing that his mother is alive, begins to search for her as frantically as she is searching for him. The danger is that with Ralph's long-postponed departure, Karel will be sucked back up into a postwar bureaucracy, killing any chance he has of finding her.

The core of *The Search* is the simple power of humanity. Children—so old before their time, so broken, yet still children—file in and out of it. One official in the film makes passing reference to a young girl who was left sorting through clothes left by those gassed at Dachau, only to find her mother's blouse. Swiss producers Lazar and David Wechsler had been sufficiently inspired by stories of such hardship and Therese Bonney's piercing photographic studies of war orphans to pitch the idea of such a film to MGM brass. The studio, impressed by the brothers' previous film, *Last Chance* (1945), put up half the $250,000 budget and agreed to get the Austrian-born Zinnemann to direct this story of cultural collision.

After Swiss writer Richard Schweizer was brought on to craft the story outline, the Wechslers and Zinnemann toured U.N.R.R.A. (United Nations Refugee Relief Association) camps in Germany, where thousands of homeless youngsters were living. Meeting ten thousand kids gave them a cadre of fifty or more to use as supporting cast, but the director and producer remained starless until an invitation to watch a group of Czech children sing at a radio station yielded the instinctive acting talent of young tenor Ivan Jandl. (His movie mom, Jarmila Novotna, also worked as an opera singer in Prague.)

What was so right about the waifish Ivan for the role of Karel? Perhaps it was the sense of sadness that underlined his wide-eyed, elfin face. Struck by infantile paralysis at age two and a half, Jandl walked with a slight defect in his left leg, which precluded his participation in any team sports. His unfamiliarity with English (like most of the real war orphans in the cast) necessitated the use of an interpreter throughout the film.

What no interpreter could have communicated was the real-life terror that broke out on the set (exteriors were filmed in Nuremberg, Munich, Frankfurt, and Würzberg) the day the children were to be moved to a new location in Red Cross ambulances, the only vehicles available in the region. It turned out that ambulances—with exhaust pipes running back into the rear cabs—were exactly what the Nazis had used to asphyxiate carloads of concentration camp prisoners who thought they were being taken to the hospital. At the sight of the vehicles, the young actors panicked and scattered until they could be convinced that the filmmakers meant no harm. This blunder was translated into the most harrowing scene in the film: Karel and other war orphans, being transported in a van, smell exhaust and bolt with tragic consequences. They have no trouble making their acting convincing.

Hollywood recognized the power of this small film and its small star with an Oscar for best motion picture story and a special prize for outstanding juvenile performance. As for Ivan, he had the business of growing up to tend to after his brief stint as a star. He continued singing and polished his English by keeping in written contact with Zinnemann, whom, for some reason, he always addressed in his postcards as "Sir Stage-Manager." One of his cards read, "Dear Sir Stage-Manager, I attend a course of English language and after vacations I wish to be a school boy of the English Grammar school. But the examinations are too unpleasant." Thank God that the war was behind him and his life was in front of him. If only it were that easy for all the others.

On the lam from an orphan's home for Holocaust survivors, ten-year-old Karel (Ivan Jandl, left) is headed for disaster and redemption in Fred Zinnemann's highly moving **The Search** *(1948).*

Chapter Five

THE KILLING GROUND

For about twenty years after the war, I couldn't look at any film on World War II. It brought back memories that I didn't want to keep around. I hated to see how it glorified war. In all those films people get blown up with their clothes and fall gracefully to the ground. You don't see anybody being blown apart. You don't see any arms and legs and mutilated bodies. You see only an antiseptic, clean, neat way to die gloriously.

—retired Rear Admiral Gene Larocque from an interview in *The Good War*, Studs Terkel's oral history of World War II

I could have looked until my lamps went out and I still wouldn't have accepted the connection between a detached leg and the rest of the body, or the poses and positions that always happened (one day I'd hear it called "response-to-impact"), bodies wrenched too fast and violently into unbelievable contortion. Or the total impersonality of group death, making them lie anywhere and any way it left them, hanging over barbed wire or thrown promiscuously on top of other dead, or up in the trees like terminal acrobats, Look what I can do.

—Vietnam combat journalist Michael Herr, from his novel *Dispatches*

Perhaps one of the best-known scenes in movie history—the massacre on the Odessa steps from Sergei Eisenstein's landmark film, The Battleship Potemkin (1925).

eath. Carnage. Chaos. Bottom line, it's what war boils down to, isn't it? From time to time movie audiences forget this little fact. The noble call of patriotism, the inhumanity of a savagely stereotyped enemy, bloodless celluloid victories, and balletically choreographed deaths often obscure it. But every once in a while a filmmaker will bring the fact home with a wallop, even in nonwar films like *Forrest Gump* (1994) and *Legends of the Fall* (1995), and renew our appreciation for the terrible cost soldiers pay for their people's freedom or their leaders' ambition.

We all know the most celebrated of war's killing grounds. Their names ring with grim familiarity—Antietam, Iwo Jima, Pork Chop Hill, Gettysburg, Omaha Beach, Bunker Hill, Hiroshima, Shiloh, the Bulge, and even Wounded Knee, the Little Big Horn, Sand Creek, and Mai Lai (and these are only some of the major conflicts where U.S. soldiers were particularly steeped in blood). When a film brings one of these legendary monuments to mortality to light or convincingly creates such a place out of myth, the results are sometimes as hard to ignore as they are to watch.

In a cinematic tide of jaunty, wise-cracking, mind-numbing, splatter-filled, adolescent action pictures, which take no responsibility for the bloodshed that they glamorize, there are still a few pearls of violence that can leave you enthralled as well as horrified.

> Lord Kurogane, at the second castle there is a supply of salt. When you bring back her head, salt it first or in this heat we'll be unable to look at it. Lady Sue is so beautiful. It would be ungracious to her.
>
> —a distinctly female flex of muscle by Lady Kaede (Mieko Harada) in Akira Kurosawa's samurai lesson in power and powerlessness, *Ran* (1985)

THE EMPEROR'S LAST BATTLE

They called him the Emperor because when he directed he was the absolute ruler of his empire. In 1985, at a venerable seventy-five years of age, Akira Kurosawa was one of the most celebrated filmmakers the world had ever produced. But whenever he was asked what his favorite film was, he always gave the same answer: "My next one." After he made his international name, brought Japanese cinema to world attention, and took home both the Grand Prize at the Venice Film Festival and the Oscar for best foreign language film with *Rashomon* (1950)—the five-way telling of a rape-murder—the director went on to overpower audiences again with his epic, three-and-a-half-hour saga of a band of sixteenth-century samurai defending a small village from bandits: *Seven Samurai* (1954). (The incredible battle scenes in the final reel, set in a whirling tempest of mud, rain, swords, horses, and death, made revolutionary use of the telephoto lens, effectively putting the flinching audience in the middle of the maelstrom.)

With his reputation for grandeur and action cemented, Kurosawa was unstoppable. He remained prolific until the late 1960s, when television's popularity led to a reduced interest in investing in big-budget movies. Producers' purse strings were so

LEFT: Victimizer (Toshiro Mifune) and victim (Miachiko Kyo) from Kurosawa's legendary Rashomon (1950), *a five-way tale of rape and murder. OPPOSITE: For beauty in bloodshed, it is impossible to outdo the master, Akira Kurosawa—especially in* Ran (1985), *his spectacular retelling of Shakespeare's* King Lear.

tight that Kurosawa was unable to raise money for the next warrior epic he had planned—*Kagemusha*. He opted not to be a gun for Hollywood hire and resigned from directing the Japanese side of the Pearl Harbor extravaganza, *Tora! Tora! Tora!* (1969).

It wasn't until foreign funding saved the day again in 1980 that *Kagemusha*, a samurai film about an impostor posing as a powerful feudal lord, was actualized thanks to Twentieth Century Fox's distribution deal (brought to reality through the lobbying of heavyweights Francis Ford Coppola and George Lucas). This film, whose title means "shadow warrior" in English, wowed audiences around the world with its epic battles (including a suicidal cavalry charge and one horrific moment with a dying horse) and scenes of stunning intimacy. Yet it was only a dress rehearsal (or so Kurosawa later said) for his twenty-seventh project—and his eleventh samurai film—*Ran* (1985), which was inspired by Shakespeare's *King Lear* and by the sixteenth-century Japanese legend of Lord Morikawa, who, like Lear, gave his kingdom to his children.

By the time Kurosawa started making this epic, he knew a good deal about age, power, and powerlessness. He had been making films for forty years but had gone unproduced in Japan since the 1970s. The word *ran* translates as "chaos," which is the antithesis of the Japanese *giri* (the structure of social obligations that binds Japanese society together—in this case, father to son and samurai to lord). The Emperor wanted this film to star Kurosawa film veteran Tatsuya Nakadai as Lord Hidetora Ichimonji, a seventy-year-old warlord (perhaps a reflection of the venerable director himself) who reaps the harvest of his own brutality when the two sons (Taro and Jiro) between whom he has divided his kingdom (while banishing his third son, Saburo) betray him, drive him insane, and eventually kill him.

Ran was huge—in length, scope, and cost. It took nine months to shoot. Eighty percent of it was shot on location at ancient castles in Nagoya, Kumamoto, and Himeji, at an active volcano on an island off Japan's south coast, and in the cities of Gotemba, Kokonoe, and Shonai. Set castles were built and destroyed. Thousands of costumed extras were needed to fight battles. Three differently sized lenses simultaneously photographed those battle scenes to get a multitude of angles and shots.

Kurosawa had a seasoned crew of regulars ready to handle all this. Screenwriter Hieo Oguni had collaborated on twelve previous scripts with the Emperor. One of his three directors of photography had worked with him since the forties. His personal assistant, Teruyo Nogami, had been at his side since the making of *Rashomon*. Even longtime aide Inoshiro Honda (famous for directing the first Godzilla films) would participate. All he needed was $11.5 million for the budget.

While he searched for producers to help with the financial end, Kurosawa executed hundreds of detailed paintings and storyboards (before studying film, he had studied art at the Proletarian Art Research Institute) for every scene in the film. In the end, venerable French producer Serge Silberman, who had produced the later films of another old master, Spanish director-writer Luis Buñuel, agreed to put together the financing for the project over a two-year period.

The masterpiece of "chaos" they created revolves around human passion, power hunger, and blood lust, and these emotions often seem like elemental forces of nature. Right from this film's start, gathering thunderheads and bloody sunsets seem to presage disaster. As the tragic story unwinds, unforgettable images first soothe, then increasingly assault the viewer. In the beginning, long grass is filmed in peaceful, undulating waves. Later that grass roils like the sea while inside a castle boudoir the widow of a slain favored son (the sensational Mieko Harada in a ghostly white Noh makeup mask of vengeance) seamlessly turns a wretched plea for mercy to her late husband's brother into an almost lethal attack, then into a feral seduction, and back once

***Kurosawa's wonderful* Seven Samurai *(1954) was the basis for the classic western* The Magnificent Seven.**

more to pitiful grief (while she squashes a bug). Finally, a typhoon rages (they filmed in an actual typhoon) while an insane, homeless Hidetora and his loyal fool (played artfully by the popular Japanese female impersonator Peter) stumble upon a man whose eyes Hidetora himself once gouged out.

The battle sequences, which divide the film roughly into three acts, are without equal. The armies of Lord Hidetora's three sons are dressed in yellow, red, and blue; the lord's soldiers wear white and gold. Fourteen hundred extras were hired to fill these stunningly embroidered costumes, but the battle sequences were filmed so skillfully that some members of the press saw as many as 120,000 soldiers. Armies of beautifully clad riders create a whirlwind of color and destruction. Archers let fly with cascades of arrows that seem like lethal rain. In the midst of it all, men are trampled and lanced with arrows, and horses are blown off their feet so convincingly that *Ran* seems like some exquisite snuff film.

Without a doubt, the most memorable scene in this constantly amazing film is the last stand of Hidetora's band of loyal samurai in an empty castle where they are trapped by one son's army. For this one scene, a full-scale castle was built at the base of Mount Fuji out of plastic, cement, and highly flammable plywood—at a cost of $1.6 million.

Inside the fort's walls, Hidetora and his remaining servants and concubines are enclosed in a high tower atop a long, steep, bannisterless stairway. As the invading army decimates the defending forces, flaming arrows pour in through the tower windows like locusts, killing most of the people inside. The women pull their ceremonial daggers and impale one another. Finally only Hidetora remains untouched, as flaming arrows practically brush his skin. He realizes the mortal toll of dividing his kingdom and quietly goes mad. As the tower starts to blaze, filling the fort with smoke and fire and necessitating a single take, a gaunt, unblinking Hidetora staggers out onto the towering steps. The battle stops as the soldiers stare in disbelief at the lord descending the flaming staircase like a sleepwalker (only kept from falling off the edge to his death by off-camera spotters). The awed crowd parts for the broken lord as he walks through them and out of the castle into the wilderness beyond.

This scene is stirring in its horror and its humanity. It seems a small touch, but the soundtrack—or lack of it—is integral to the effect. Only when the hush is broken by a gunshot do you realize that there has been no sound during this moment other than Toru Takemitsu's sumptuous and melancholy musical scoring. *Ran* has that kind of simple, terrible beauty.

If Kurosawa's place in the pantheon of film greats was not already secure, *Ran*, with its insights into age and bloody chaos, ensured that the director could not be forgotten. The tributes that rained in like arrows soon after the film's release were small consolation for the death of his sound man, his fight director, and his beloved wife of forty years during the filming. But now, when the Emperor was asked what his favorite film was, he had a new answer: *Ran*.

CRY "GOD FOR HARRY, ENGLAND AND SAINT GEORGE...AND A PERCENTAGE OF THE GROSS!"

During the darkest days of World War II, the theater's golden boy, Laurence Olivier, captured the hearts of millions with his shining tribute to British patriotism, *Henry V* (1943). With its lofty speeches, dashing leading man, and wonderful costumes, this movie, based on the play by William Shakespeare, was like something out of a story-book: magical, lyrical and, for a war movie, distinctly bloodless. More than forty years later, another golden boy was on the rise.

> *All the eyewitnesses of Agincourt and Harfleur tell a story much more gritty and bloody than even we have described, with dysentery rife and an incredible stench and sensational brutality. French bodies piled 6 feet [1.8m] high, with most of them dying of suffocation in the crush, and wild Irishmen ripping off their clothes and running into battle naked in the filth. Terrible, unbelievable.*
>
> —actor-director Kenneth Branagh on his *Henry V* (1989)

Brought up in volatile Belfast and introduced to Shakespeare by a high school English teacher who had plumbed *Romeo and Juliet* for sexual innuendos and puns, Kenneth Branagh had grown up to cofound the fabulously successful Renaissance Theater Company. He also had the unmitigated gall to publish an autobiography, *Beginnings*, at the age of twenty-eight. In 1989, with only three other films to his acting credit (and none under his belt as a director), Kenneth Branagh launched into a project that must have seemed insane to those around him: he would redo everybody's favorite Shakespeare film of the young king who made medieval history fighting France.

Branagh wanted to make his *Henry V* ring with reality. He also wanted to make "a popular film that would satisfy the Shakespearean scholars as well as the filmgoers who like *Crocodile Dundee* [1986]." Olivier's film had omitted untidy scenes like the king's early betrayal by boyhood friends on the eve of war (whom he punishes with execution) and the hanging of Bardolph (a beloved rogue from Henry's misspent youth) for stealing from a French church during battle. Branagh wanted them back in and more. He wanted to give the Battle of Agincourt its due.

On October 25, 1415 (Saint Crispin's Day), six thousand wet and exhausted British soldiers (most of them armed with longbows) attacked twenty-five thousand heavily armed French and somehow won the day. The battle was a bloodbath and the cost to the French was tremendous.

For two years Branagh and producer (and cofounder of the Renaissance Theater Company) Stephen Evans looked for a way to bring Henry's army back to life. Not many studios wanted to invest the $8 million plus to make it a go, but Branagh had wisely cultivated some heavy hitters. Several years before, he had invited reigning English stage stars like Judi Dench, Paul Scofield, and Ian Holm to try their hand at directing for his hot young theater company. It was the perfect way to forge a working relationship

and show them his own talent as an actor. He had also befriended numerous actors and played Henry onstage at the Royal Shakespeare Company's Stratford stage. His pug-faced, unglamorous portrayal was phenomenally successful for the very reason that, unlike Olivier, he wasn't "a decisive and resolved king in a shining armored image" but on a much "less certain journey toward maturity." Here was a Henry you could worry about.

As Branagh wined and dined stars in an effort to get them to appear in his film (should it ever be made) and worked on adapting his screenplay, he and Evans spent a part of each day contacting potential backers. On what must have been a stroke of genius or madness, Branagh wangled a brief interview with one of the biggest backers imaginable: Prince Charles. All he really wanted was to get some insight into the royal mind-set; what he got was much more. Charles was taken with the young upstart and in addition to imparting to Branagh the sense of isolation and responsibility that accompanies royal privilege, he extended their chat into a three-hour conversation and offered to be a royal booster for the production.

With enough backing to lure the Samuel Goldwyn Company to pick up the tab, Branagh went to work. He knew what he wanted and when he didn't know how to get it, he unhesitatingly asked his production crew. There was also on-the-job training when it came to acting. The film featured a stellar cast that included Derek Jacobi, Brian Blessed, Judi Dench, Christian Bale, and Emma

"Once more down to the beach, dear friends." Laurence Olivier's storybook **Henry V** *(1943), above, was a Sunday picnic compared to what upstart Kenneth Branagh would do with it forty-six years later in his grittier, blood-soaked* **Henry V** *(1989), left.*

Thompson. Three of these actors—Ian Holm (the wild Welshman Fluellen), Paul Scofield (the French king), and Michael Williams (Williams)—had played Henry before. They watched the young actor-director carefully and their advice, unasked for and perhaps unintended certainly was a factor in Branagh's choices. Branagh later said, "Ian never interfered or anything, but I'd do four or five takes and he'd just kind of wink and say, 'That's the one' out of the side of his mouth, and I'd realize, oh-oh! That's an unofficial tip. So, I'd print that one."

Branagh's Henry is a gritty combination of valiant soldier and future statesman. He awakes his "sleeping sword of war" with complete understanding of its grim consequences. He replies to conveyed taunts from the French Dauphin (prince) with equal parts simple soldier's scorn and king's lacerating wit. He appreciates and shares the deprivations that his unschooled troops face in the French rain and mud.

During a pause in the battle for the besieged town of Harlfleur, Branagh is terrifyingly convincing and pained as he urges the men of the town to surrender while his "blind and bloody" troops are still under his control or face the consequences, which include "foul hands" defiling the locks of "shrill-shrieking daughters," grabbing the silver beards of old men and smashing "their most reverend heads" against the wall, and impaling naked infants on pikes while "mad mothers with their howls confused do break the clouds." He gets his point across.

But Harlfleur isn't the end of it. Branagh's Henry prowls his camp in disguise to assess his men's doubts and dread on the night before the fabled Battle of Agincourt. He prays to God to quiet his own fears. And with noble words as the next day dawns, Branagh's Henry works himself and his troops into a killing frenzy that you might expect from a pack of animals.

The Battle of Agincourt is a sight to behold. As the inimitable movie lover, critic, and sometime screenwriter Roger Ebert has said, it is a war not of words "but of swords." There are trenches. There is mud. There is rain. And there is more killing than you can imagine. Some critics fault the film for the slow-motion violence, but the grim hand-to-hand combat is mesmerizing. Olivier took nine weeks to shoot his Agincourt. Branagh had nine days. Wedged on a plain near Sheperton Studios between a housing project and power lines, he was forced to shoot many scenes in close-up, which made the slaughter that much more intimate.

When the smoke clears (Branagh created the cloaking backdrop of a bilious gray sky with hundreds of smoke grenades), Henry, like all his surviving men, is exhausted and unclear as to the outcome: "I know not if the day be ours or no." When told by the French herald Mountjoy (Christopher Ravenscroft) not only that he is the victor, but that ten thousand French lie dead, compared to a scant twenty-five Englishmen (a slight exaggeration on Shakespeare's part), he breaks down into a combination of laughter and weeping in the arms of his Welsh cousin. Like the king, we in the audience are spent, and like him we delight in the genteel denouement of this fine film. We've both earned it.

WAR'S RUSHED RUSSIAN MASTERPIECE

In 1958, at the International Exhibition in Brussels, film critics and historians from all over the world were polled as to what picture deserved that most inflated title, "best film of all time." To 117 of them from twenty-six different countries, the answer was clear: Sergei Eisenstein's silent homage to unity over brutality, *The Battleship Potemkin* (1925). Charlie Chaplin, who is often pegged as the grand wazoo of moviemakers, called it "the best film in the world." Today, there are many film aficionados and critics who would agree with that bold statement. As recently as 1982, *The Battleship Potemkin* was ranked #6 in the fourth International Critics' Poll.

What's all the hoopla about? Eisenstein, the filmmaker who showed the world what quickly cut, carefully interposed images (a/k/a montage) could do for dynamic storytelling on film, never showed it better than in this beautiful, imagistic war movie. Though this visual genius was accused in his day of distorting truth and rewriting history in a documentary-style format to serve his nefarious, dramatic purposes (Oliver Stone might relate), his movie remains amazing. And what may be most amazing is the speed with which he made it.

On March 19, 1925, the Commission for the Twentieth Anniversary of the 1905 Revolution hired a handful of directors to create film tributes. One of these filmmakers was a twenty-seven-year-old whiz kid with unruly hair who had made only one other film—*Strike* (1924), a visually stunning tribute to collective action that starred the entire Moscow Worker's Theater. The former engineer and proletariat theater director started out with a less than modest plan; a film entitled *The Year of 1905*, which he cowrote with a revolutionary named Nina Agadzhanova-Shutko. This movie was to chronicle the entire year of revolutionary events in as many as thirty towns and cities. And it had to be ready by the end of the year.

With a several-hundred-page manuscript in hand, Eisenstein and crew (including his cameraman, Eduard Tisse) began filming in Leningrad in July. Unfortunately (or perhaps, fortunately, as it turned out) summer rains made filming impossible, and Eisenstein retreated to the Lenin Library to dry out, brood, and do research. In the course of his research, the director happened upon an article from a Paris magazine called *L'Illustration* that told of a sailors' mutiny aboard the battleship Potemkin. This mutiny over inhumane conditions (specifically, maggoty meat) spread ashore through sympathies between the people and the sailors, and became a bloody rebellion over human rights in the port city of Odessa (ironic, since the czar's ship was there to keep such an event from occurring).

Intrigued, our captain led his crew to the port, where he paced up and down the magnificent cascade of one hundred steps leading to its harbor. More inspired with each lap, Eisenstein had soon chucked all his pages except the two that already happened to be on the mutiny and changed his filmic course (and many a film course) from sweeping history to a crystallized essence of the entire revolution as seen in one explosive moment.

His story followed the unrest from nautical mistreatment to sailors on strike, to punitive execution, to soldiers refusing to fire on sailors, to mutiny, to the fall of a hero, to a whole town mourning, to a whole town revolting, to Cossacks killing the townsfolk on the steps (in one of the most harrowing scenes of cinematic slaughter ever, which, in truth, was a composite of several other massacres), to the sailor-seized battleship firing on the Cossacks, to the entire Russian fleet coming to sink the ship, to...well, it was enough to make a capitalist action-picture director's head spin.

In the course of the filming, however, many problems arose. For instance, the only available battleship was *The Twelve Apostles*, which was moored and rusting hundreds of miles away in Sevastopol, was missing some of its superstructure (which Eisenstein filled in with wood) and had a cargo hold full of old mines. So instead of moving the ship to the cast, the cast moved to the ship and no smoking was allowed on the set.

Amateur actors were fine for *The Battleship Potemkin*, for there was no hero—just humanity and the event. To capture the moment, the director shot like a madman, putting as many as seventy-five shots a day in the can. Each day after filming (whether on board the ship or in Odessa), the next day's scenes were rehearsed before dinner, with each of Eisenstein's hungry assistant directors

You don't need sounds to put audiences on the edge of their seats—not if you have sights like this one from **The Battleship Potemkin** *(1925). Somebody stop that baby carriage!*

walking through the part of his group of a hundred or more extras in a wondrous mise-en-scène, while their leader frantically barked orders and made revisions in his shooting script. Despite all this preparation, the great navigator never limited himself to one particular course once the filming started the next morning.

Making the most of the inspiration of the moment brought much gold to this golden film. The sickening descent of baby and carriage down Odessa's steps to the water after a Cossack's kick—one of the most celebrated moments in film and one which Brian DePalma shamelessly "borrowed" in *The Untouchables* (1989)—was completely spur-of-the-moment. A chance visit to Odessa's Alupka Palace yielded the image (furtively shot by Eisenstein while he was being chased around the palace grounds by its guard) of three stone lions—in poses of sleep, wakening, and rage—that came to symbolize the oppressed masses. A shot taken aboard the fogbound ship one morning became a chilling, funereally shrouded statement of mourning for the butchered sailors.

The cinema can make a far bigger contribution and a far stronger impression by projecting matter and bodies rather than feelings. We photograph an echo and the rat-tat-tat of a machine gun. The impression is physiological. Our approach is, on the one hand, that of the great Russian scholar, Pavlov, with his principles of reflexology, and on the other, that of the Austrian, Freud—the principle of psychoanalysis.

Take the scene in Potemkin *where Cossacks slowly, deliberately, walk down the Odessa steps firing into the masses....The spectator does not imagine himself at the Odessa wharf in 1905. But as the soldiers' boots press forward, he physically recoils. He tries to get out of the range of bullets. As the baby carriage goes over the side of the mole, he holds on to his cinema chair. He does not want to fall into the water.*

—S.M. Eisenstein, writing in The Nation *(1927)*

Even Eisenstein's use of his throngs of extras was improvisational. He energized them for the slaughter on the steps by randomly calling out direction to likely Russian names that came into his head. That way, all the extras felt that the director was watching individual performances (which he couldn't possibly have done). At one point, however, his direction became a tad too inventive: after having coordinated ships in Odessa harbor to fire on his signal, he was asked by a visiting naval officer how he could possibly synchronize all the action. "Oh, quite simple," he replied. "I'll take my handkerchief from my pocket and wave it three times." He demonstrated. So did the ships, and a fleet's worth of cannon shell blanks was wasted.

By hook and by crook, Eisenstein made his masterpiece in record time. Shooting was finished in a scant seven weeks—from late September to early November—and the director was left with 50,000 feet (15,240m) of film that had to be cut down to 5,000 feet (1,524m) in a scant seventeen more days. (And with all those beautiful, horrifying images, Eisenstein found it extremely difficult to decide what to cut.) Working around the clock, he cut it himself and, true to form, was working on the titles (which he wrote and selected fonts for) up until the film's first screening in Moscow on December 21, 1925. In fact, he was riding to the theater on the back of a friend's motorcycle with the freshly completed last reel when their bike broke down—just as the curtain was going up on the first reel. Eisenstein sprinted the last half-mile (0.8km) to the theater. Thanks to the fact that reels were still being projected one at a time (as opposed to being set up and waiting on two alternating projectors), he made it with time to spare. And the audience was none the wiser.

WHAT PRICE GLORY?

During the Civil War, as many as 700,000 Americans died in combat. This is more than half the number of Americans killed in all the wars in which the country has played a role. While fifty thousand died during the fifteen years of the Vietnam War, forty thousand died during the five hours of the Battle of Antietam. The War Between the States was no high-tech affair or guerrilla war, but an often point-blank conflict of cannons, muskets, and bayonets that was almost incomprehensible in its capacity for slaughter. It was not unusual for soldiers to march toward their enemies a stone's throw away with both sides firing in each other's faces.

American citizens of African descent have fought for this country since the Revolution, often in highly decorated all-black units from the War Between the States through the Korean War's 24th Infantry Regiment. Not many people know that 186,107 free men of color (12 percent of the Union Army) fought in 449 battles during the "War to Free the Slaves" or that black men made up 25 percent of the Union Navy (thirty thousand men). And they did not serve only as soldiers—200,000 more African Americans served as scouts, carpenters, laborers, and cooks. More than thirty-seven thousand blacks lost their lives defending the Union. Seventeen were awarded the Congressional Medal of Honor for heroism. It is widely

It may not look it, but Colonel Robert Gould Shaw (Matthew Broderick) has the best material in the world to transform into a valiant regiment of fighting men in Glory (1989).

believed by historians that their involvement helped turn the tide for the Union. But none of this would have happened had it not been for one group of men—the 4th Regiment of the Massachusetts Volunteer Infantry.

Along one wall of the Boston Common, opposite the State House, there is a massive bronze statue created by Augustus Saint-Gaudens that depicts a twenty-five-year-old white Boston colonel, Robert Gould Shaw, riding at the head of a column of black volunteer infantrymen on their way to one of the bloodiest battles of the war. These men are headed for an attack that they pray will pave the way for the taking of Charleston, South Carolina (where the war began at Fort Sumter)—an attack on the highly defended rebel stronghold of Fort Wagner on Morris Island. They have labored long and hard for the right to prove themselves in battle. Based on their heroism, sixty more all-black regiments will be added to the Union Army by the end of the year. Still, for almost half their number, the only reward will be everlasting glory.

Lincoln Kirstein, the venerable director of the New York City Ballet, was also a dyed-in-the-wool Bostonian—and a Civil War buff to boot. The Saint-Gaudens monument had long inspired him. He had even written the text for a series of photographs of it called *Lay This Laurel.*

When Kirstein was summering in Saratoga, New York, he happened to see a picture of Kevin Jarre, the stepson of famed film composer Maurice, on horseback. Kirstein immediately noted the young writer's resemblance to Robert Gould Shaw. Arranging a meeting with the young writer, he told him all about the statue and the story. Shortly after this meeting, Jarre, who had been a Civil War enthusiast since being given lead soldiers as a little boy, sequestered himself for four weeks in Room 421 of New York's Gramercy Park Hotel and wrote a script called *Glory.* (He used a number of books, including Kirstein's text for the photographs and Peter Burchard's *One Gallant Rush,* as well as Shaw's letters to his family, as source material).

Hitting the beach, Civil War style. Most of these brave men (the officers and an all-black regiment) are about to die for Glory (1989).

Once the script was done, it was shown to director Bruce Beresford (*Breaker Morant*, 1979, *Crimes of the Heart*, 1986, and *Driving Miss Daisy*, 1989), who in turn brought it to producer Freddie Fields. The producer shopped it around, but the story left most studio executives cold. As if a movie about the Civil War wasn't bad enough, this one was about black soldiers in the Civil War, fighting a battle that they got creamed in. And with the recent flak that *Mississippi Burning* (1988) and Alan Parker had gotten for telling a black story using white heroes, Hollywood didn't want to make another racial mistake. But Fields and director Edward Zwick, the cocreator of television's *Thirtysomething* didn't give up easily. They arranged for a second unit crew to make a nine-minute film on Antietam using footage of fifteen hundred Civil War buffs recreating Pickett's infamous charge at Gettysburg. After being shown this short, executives at Tristar finally saw the action potential in *Glory.* For despite its perspective—events are seen through the eyes of the twenty-five-year-old Shaw (played by twenty-five-year-old Matthew Broderick)—the film is really about a group of black heroes and their rugged journey to the ultimate sacrifice.

While there were approximately twelve hundred troops in Shaw's regiment, the script focuses on four tentmates: John Rawlins (Morgan Freeman), a gravedigger whom Gould first met on the battlefield of Antietam; Jupiter Sharts (Jihmi Kennedy), a gentle, squirrel-hunting Carolina kid; Thomas Searles (Andre Braugher), a bespectacled and sophisticated childhood friend of Shaw's; and Trip (Denzel Washington), a runaway slave with more than his share of anger.

This fine film, shot almost entirely in Georgia (even the Boston sequences), follows the regiment from its creation to its grueling training at Readville, Massachusetts, under a tyrannical Irish sergeant (John Joseph Finn) who refers to them as "Hindus," to Beaufort, South Carolina, and their first fight against the rebels on the Georgia border, to their assault on Fort Wagner.

The movie is filled with personal moments, as Shaw and his men learn from one another on their way to battle. There is the marksman Shart's brutal lesson in speed firing, given to him by Shaw; the dandified Searles' tests of manhood; Trip's punishment for desertion (during which Denzel Washington's face tells a story beyond words); surprising solidarity in confronting army racism; the regimental prayer meeting around the campfire the night before the attack on Fort Wagner; and Shaw's final gesture of brotherhood before the onslaught.

Then there is the warfare. Historical accuracy had been of the utmost importance throughout the ten-week shoot—fifteen hundred fully costumed fanatical Civil War re-creators had seen to that. Civil War historian Shelby Foote had already combed over Jarre's script to take out twentieth-century war terms like "over the top" and ensure that details such as right and left shoes being identical weren't overlooked. The underside of the Union caps were tinted a historical green (though the camera never sees the bottoms of the caps). In fact, the only inaccuracies that firearms expert Russ Pritchard and flag collector Stan Smulen could find in the film were the facts that serial numbers are called out for the Enfield rifles (army rifles didn't have serial numbers back then) and that the stars were sewn on Old Glory (they were painted on the flag at the time).

Combat expert B.H. Barry kept a careful eye on the recreation of the 54th's suicidal July 18, 1863, charge against Fort Wagner. Though fifty Union warships had bombarded the fort for days, the bluecoats' ratio to their enemy did not stack up two-to-one, as Shaw and his troops had believed, but was, in fact, a staggering one-to-three. With full knowledge of both Jefferson Davis' 1862 edict that Negro "soldiers" in Union uniform would immediately be put to death if captured and the 1863 decision of the Confederate Congress to allot the same fate to the white officers leading them, the 54th attempted the 800 feet (243.8m) of hell across open sand and up the steep walls of the fort.

It is harrowing to watch these men you have come to care so deeply about in the battle that they so passionately wanted to "ante into," as Rawlins put it. Night flares illuminate troops blown skyward by cannon blasts. Bayonets plunge and twist. One by one, the patriots prove their mettle and meet their maker. And it all seems that much more tragic with the voices of the Boys Choir of Harlem behind it. The aftermath, with its eerie peace, is one of the most powerful images of brotherhood ever screened.

> White Americans are still...trapped in a history which they do not understand; and until they understand it, they cannot be released from it.
>
> —author James Baldwin

The African-American soldiers in **Glory** *(1989) proved their worth in their very first skirmish.*

DREAM A LITTLE DREAM OF ME

Fighting and waiting to fight—life on the battlefield. With so much unremitting stress and tension, soldiers needed something more pleasant than their next maneuver to focus on—they needed escape, preferably into sexual fantasy. And during World War II, Hollywood (with its stars and starlets) was happy to provide it. Postcards, photographs, and pinups of scantily clad women in bathing suits, negligees, and short shorts jumping out of candy boxes, carving Thanksgiving turkeys, and riding Santa's sleigh—you name the pose and you could find it decorating a trench, barracks, or the inside of a helmet. Some starlets, such as Yvonne De Carlo (later of the television show The Munsters*), got their start in Hollywood dishing out cheesecake as a pinup girl. Some established stars cemented their sex appeal in the same way. Betty Grable became so heavily identified with her poses that her daughter with bandleader Harry James was quickly dubbed "Little Pin Up" by the press. Men even went into combat armed with their dream girls. During the Burma campaign, one tank tangoed into battle with a 5-foot (1.5m) cutout of Ginger Rogers wired to its front. Rita Hayworth's bombshell, Gilda, became the real thing when the name was painted on the side of the atomic bomb tested off the Bikini atoll after the war. Here are a few classic WWII images of erotica brought to us by the ladies who were kind enough to objectify themselves for the cause.*

- *A plateful of Evelyn Keys got the moniker "Miss Tastiest Dish"*

- *The voluptuous Marilyn Monroe was voted "The Girl We'd Most Like to Examine" by the Medical Corps of the Army's 7th Division*

- *Susan Hayward was dubbed "Miss Everything Except Miss Take" by her admirers*

- *Yvonne De Carlo was "The Sweetheart of the U.S. Mechanized Forces"*

- *The most famous of all WWII pinups was an afterthought on Miss Grable's part. She should have considered herself lucky. Her photographer had previously photographed Carmen Miranda twirling in a flared skirt that revealed that she wasn't wearing any panties.*

Hubba-hubba! What'll it be, soldier? Pierside with Miss Yvonne De Carlo (above left) or bedside with Miss Rita Hayworth (above)?

FOR THE BOYS

The son of a New York stockbroker, Oliver Stone had dropped out of Yale in 1965, taught English, history, and mathematics to Chinese students in Vietnam for six months, and taken a tour with the merchant marine before he volunteered for the infantry in Vietnam. He later claimed, "It was my way of announcing to my father that I was a man." Enlisting was also his way of repenting for having had the chutzpah to write a book on his Vietnam teaching and merchant marine experiences (which, as it turned out, nobody wanted). "I had to atone for that act of individuality. So I had to become a common soldier. I had to have my hair cut. I had to be a number," Stone has said.

He certainly got his wish for anonymity. On his twenty-first birthday, Stone was in flight to join the 25th Infantry near the Cambodian border, where he saw action within the first two weeks. During his tour in Vietnam, Stone served with three different companies, was wounded twice, and received the Bronze Star and Purple Heart for bravery. He also came back with a need to tell the story of how the war that he went to fight was nothing like he thought it would be.

He attended New York University to learn how to write and direct that story for film. He graduated in 1971, and soon discovered that no one wanted to hear his tale. Though his directorial debut, a Canadian horror film called *Seizure* (1974), was no glittering success, Stone's screenplay for *Midnight Express* (1978), William Hays' true story of imprisonment for drug smuggling in Turkey and his eventual escape, earned Stone an Oscar in 1978. In 1986 Stone came out with *Salvador*, an excellent tale of journalists under fire in Central America that he directed and cowrote. This film inspired

Hemdale Films to back the Vietnam project that Stone had been waiting ten years to do. It would be as much a tribute to the young men who lost their lives "in country" as it was an acknowledgment of the atrocities that became commonplace there (in this movie, almost every horrible thing that can happen to a group of grunts does happen). *Platoon* (1986) broke the silence and broke the mold.

In the history of film, warfare has generally been presented as a rational thing. There were slaughters and massacres, but fighting usually had an organized strategy behind it—a spar for a soldier's sanity. In Stone's experience, however, this was simply not the case. He had seen too many jungle-smothered, fear-crazed boys "rock and roll" crazily at a fleeting shadow. He had seen too many die just when they thought they were safe. To show those hard facts, he put an ensemble of novice screen actors through some of the most grueling training ever done in the name of actor preparation.

REMEMBER, IT'S ONLY A MOVIE

Stone almost didn't get to make his movie. Over the years, many countries have served as film surrogates for Vietnam. *The Lost Command* (1966) was filmed in Spain, *The Green Berets* (1968) in Georgia, *Who'll Stop the Rain* (1978) in Mexico, *Uncommon Valor* (1983) in Hawaii, *The Boat People* (1983) in China, *Missing in Action*

A very green Charlie Sheen about to enter that hell called "in country," where he will lose his ideals and maybe even his life, in Oliver Stone's Platoon *(1986).*

II—The Beginning (1985) on the Virgin Island of St. Kitts, *Full Metal Jacket* (1987) in jolly old England, *Strike Commando* (1987) in Italy, *Bat 21* (1988) in Malaysia, *Distant Thunder* (1988) in Canada, *Casualties of War* (1989) in Thailand, *In Country* (1989) in Kentucky, and *The Iron Triangle* (1989) in Sri Lanka. Stone had the bad timing to pick the Philippines.

At first, the presidential elections in the Philippines made things a tad too real. With executions carried out by Ferdinand Marcos' thugs and Corazon Aquino supporters ready to revolt, it looked like the islands could be headed for a civil war of their own. Five of Stone's actors pulled out at the last moment (undoubtedly, to their everlasting regret), but with the dictator's flight in February 1986 and Aquino's takeover, things were back on track.

Stone enlisted the services of retired marine captain Dale Dye, along with three of Dye's marine reservist aides, to train thirty actors while steeping them in the correct amount of combat profanity and lingo. Dye admitted, "I set up a training course that was intentionally difficult and physically demanding. I believe the only way a man can portray the rigors of jungle combat is to get a taste of it." And so for Charlie Sheen (the film's narrator, Chris, who is based on Stone himself), Forrest Whitaker (the sweet-natured Big Harold), Francesco Quinn (the macho Rhah), Richard Edson (the lost Sal), Kevin Dillon (the trigger-happy punk, Bunny), John C. McGinley (the swaggering coward, Sergeant O'Neill), Mark Moses (the inept and privileged Lieutenant Wolfe), Johnny Depp

I figured that after two or three hours in the field, we'd go back to our barracks to shower, rehearse and have a hot, catered meal. I couldn't have been more wrong! We came as close as we could to the real thing without anyone shooting at us.

—Charlie Sheen, on the preparation for *Platoon*

Oliver Stone back in Vietnam to make **Platoon** *(1986), his paean to the fighting man.*

(Lerner), Reggie Johnson (Junior), Keith David (King), David Neirdorf (Tex), Tony Todd (Warren), and eighteen others...thirteen days of HELL began.

After their 60-mile (97km) ride from the Manila airport to the bush, each actor was issued fatigues, boots, helmet, dog tags, rifles, bayonets, ponchos with liners, flashlights (with red filters for night use), four canteens, and heavy packs laden with other supplies. The cast slept in two-man foxholes, which they bloodied their palms and blistered their hands digging (occasionally with mock mortar fire going on around them). They slept each night on 50/50 alerts—each man would stand guard for two hours and then sleep for two hours (as well as he could with biting red ants crawling over him).

Roll call was bright and early each day at 5 A.M. and daily training included classes on operating an M-16 (always emphasizing the danger of blanks), squad radio procedures (never say "over and out"), scene study, and character analysis. With humid temperatures running over 100°F (38°C), days were also spent on full-gear slogs—the last of which was 11.2 miles (18km)—over the rugged, jungle terrain. One overnight hump left the actors lost and disoriented until they scaled a sheer rock wall and found their way out.

For physical toughening they practiced exercises like "The Stomp," where they ran in place for hours at a time, and "The Punch," in which they practiced pummeling one another in the guts. Hygiene consisted of taking sponge baths with water from their helmets. Food was cold rations twice a day (ready-to-eat approximations of hot dogs, hamburgers, and beans) with even yummier C-rations saved for filming.

The actors who played the opposing-archetype sergeants between which the men in *Platoon* are torn—Tom Berenger as the scar-faced cutthroat Barnes (whose character was based on a sergeant of Stone's who had actually been shot in the face and returned to duty) and Willem Dafoe as the Christlike Elias—arrived even earlier for leadership training. Dafoe remembers that during the training,"I became compulsively concerned about my men. I wanted to be sure they were ready day or night—for anything that happened." Because of the hours of makeup needed to create his horrible facial scars (using materials used for prosthetic devices for amputees), Berenger had to begin his workday even before the dawn call. He recalls that they were all run so ragged during the two weeks of training that "by the time the cameras rolled, we all had the thousand-yard stare."

The actors went straight from graduation to filming in the rain forest without a break. As Stone said, "The idea of the cram course was to immerse the actors into the infantryman's life, his way of thinking, talking, and moving. I hoped that subconsciously what would slip out would be the dog-tired, don't-give-a-damn attitude, the anger, frustration, casual brutality and the way death was approached. I remember being so tired that I wished the NVA [North Vietnamese Army] would come up and shoot me and get things over with."

Whatever the motivation, the training paid off. The men in *Platoon* are some of the most believably frightened, exhausted, angry, stoned, paranoid, lost boys ever to scorch the face of the earth. There is no plot, just the headlong, crazed rush of events the platoon undergoes and the confrontation between the stoner Elias and the savage Barnes after a massacre that smacks of Mai Lai. Stone may have been criticized here (as in other films) for filming fiction in a way that screams fact, but he has also given audiences a first glimpse into a world where nothing makes sense, where nowhere is safe—an unfiltered view of the killing ground.

MIXED CONFLICTS,
OR, NAME THAT PLATOON

Each of the following films tells a story about a specific war, battle, or uprising. See if you're enough of a warrior to match the title with the conflict it chronicles.

THE WAR

1. Anglo-Saxon Rebellions (1066–1174)
2. Indonesian Civil War (1965)
3. War of 1812 (1812–1814)
4. Afghanistan War (1979)
5. Russian Revolution (1917)
6. Napoleonic Wars (1803–1815)
7. Hundred Years' War (1337–1457)
8. Crimean War (1854–1856)
9. Apache Wars (1871–1876)
10. Greek Civil War (1944–1949)
11. South African Apartheid (1977)
12. Texas War of Independence (1836)
13. Algerian War (1954–1962)
14. Anglo-Spanish Wars (1587–1729)
15. French Revolution (1789–1799)
16. Sudanese War (1896–1899)
17. Sino-Japanese War (1937–1945)
18. Roman Civil Wars (49–31 B.C.)
19. Boer War (1899–1902)
20. Spanish-American War (1898)
21. Mexican Revolution (1910–1921)
22. American Civil War (1861–1865)
23. Abenaki Wars (1675–1725)
24. Sioux Wars (1862–1891)
25. The Crusades (1095–1291)
26. Comanche Wars (1858–1866)
27. Australian Convict Revolts (1800s)
28. Irish Rebellion (1960s)
29. Glorious Revolution (1688–1689)
30. French and Indian War (1754–1763)
31. Russo-Turkish War (1877–1878)
32. Spanish Civil War (1936–1939)
33. Arab-Israeli War (1948–1949)
34. American Revolution (1775–1783)
35. Cheyenne Wars (1864–1878)
36. Cuban Revolution (1956–1959)
37. Boxer Rebellion (China) (1900)
38. Bear Flag Republic (California) Revolt (1846)
39. Khmer Rouge Takeover of Cambodia (1970)
40. Nicaraguan Civil War (1979)
41. Russo-Finnish War (1939–1940)

THE MOVIE

A: A Tale of Two Cities *(1936)*
B: The Rough Riders *(1927)*
C: Cry Freedom *(1987)*
D: Ivanhoe *(1952)*
E: Rambo III *(1988)*
F: Captain Fury *(1939)*
G: Kit Carson *(1940)*
H: Saint Joan *(1957)*
I: In the Name of the Father *(1992)*
J: Flying Tigers *(1942)*
K: Cleopatra *(1963)*
L: Viva Zapata! *(1952)*
M: For Whom the Bell Tolls *(1943)*
N: The Alamo *(1960)*
O: Desiree *(1954)*
P: The Buccaneer *(1958)*
Q: The Killing Fields *(1984)*
R: Geronimo *(1962)*
S: Conquest of Cochise *(1953)*
T: The Charge of the Light Brigade *(1936)*
U: Forty-Five Days at Peking *(1963)*
V: Che! *(1969)*
W: Captain Blood *(1935)*
X: The Light That Failed *(1939)*
Y: The Four Feathers *(1929)*
Z: Under Fire *(1983)*
AA: They Died With Their Boots On *(1941)*
BB: The Year of Living Dangerously *(1983)*
CC: Journey to Shiloh *(1968)*
DD: Drums Along the Mohawk *(1939)*
EE: Sword of the Desert *(1949)*
FF: Lost Command *(1966)*
GG: The Sea Hawk *(1940)*
HH: Eleni *(1985)*
II: Last of the Mohicans *(1992)*
JJ: Doctor Zhivago *(1965)*
KK: Ski Patrol *(1940)*
LL: The Soldier and the Lady *(1937)*
MM: White Feather *(1955)*
NN: The Saracen Blade *(1954)*
OO: Northwest Passage *(1940)*

Answers

1=D, 2=BB, 3=P, 4=E, 5=JJ, 6=O, 7=H, 8=T, 9=R, 10=HH, 11=C, 12=N, 13=FF, 14=GG, 15=A, 16=Y, 17=I, 18=K, 19=X, 20=B, 21=L, 22=CC, 23=OO, 24=AA, 25=NN, 26=S, 27=F, 28=I, 29=W, 30=II, 31=LL, 32=M, 33=EE, 34=DD, 35=MM, 36=V, 37=U, 38=G, 39=Q, 40=Z, 41=KK

Chapter Six

THE CRY FOR PEACE

War is mostly long periods of boredom punctuated by terrifying seconds of madness and surrealism.

—director Oliver Stone

Nobody yet has made a good anti-war picture because we still have wars.

—director René Clair

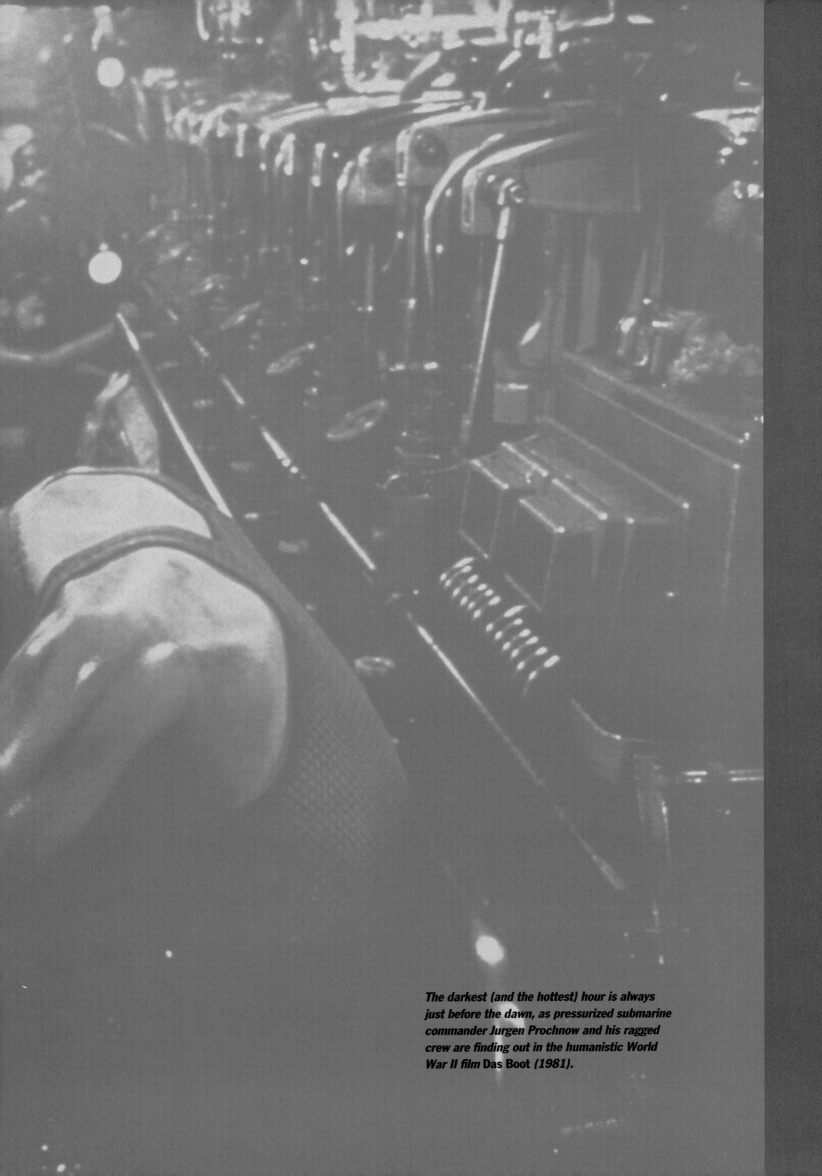

The darkest (and the hottest) hour is always just before the dawn, as pressurized submarine commander Jurgen Prochnow and his ragged crew are finding out in the humanistic World War II film Das Boot *(1981).*

For as long as war has been glorified, it has also been deplored. The wisest people in the world have spent considerable time, energy, and eloquence trying to talk humanity out of its baser nature. In the Book of Isaiah, men are told to "beat their swords into plowshares, and their spears into pruning hooks" in order that they "not lift up sword against nation" and not "learn war anymore." Rome's Cicero said, *"Cedant arma togae, concedant laurae laudi"* ("Let war yield to peace, laurels to paeans"). In more modern times, Ben Franklin wisely wrote, "There never was a good war, or a bad peace." Oscar Wilde gave war-bashing his usual bad-boy spin, saying, "As long as war is regarded as wicked, it will always have its fascination. When it is looked upon as vulgar, it will cease to be popular." Even the roaring English lion Sir Winston Churchill admitted that "to jaw-jaw is better than to war-war."

Artists haven't been asleep through all this lecturing. Sure, Shakespeare may have glorified a battle or two in plays like *Henry V* and *Richard II* (after all, the butter for his bread often came in the form of commissions from the government). Alfred, Lord Tennyson went half-a-league half-a-league half-a-league onward through the Valley of Death to immortalize "The Charge of the Light Brigade." Stephen Crane scored big with his novel *The Red Badge of Courage* (1895), a paean to patriotism and battlefield heroics (though he had never actually been in a battle). But poet Walt Whitman, who had lived on the battlefield, nursing dying soldiers in blue and gray, translated the grisly reality of his Civil War experiences into a book of poems, *Drum Taps* (1865). And Ralph Waldo Emerson, Leo Tolstoy, Bertrand Russell, and Mahatma Gandhi all wrote eloquently and prolifically for peace.

After the horrors of the large-scale slaughter on the battlefields of World War I, many more artists reassessed the glory of war, many of them filmmakers. One of the earliest and most powerful was American cinema patriarch D.W. Griffith, who had vilified and stereotyped Germans to a fare-thee-well in the prewar silent *Hearts of the World* (1918), which starred "the man you love to hate"—monocled actor Erich Von Stroheim. With the defeated Germany left destitute after the armistice that officially brought World War I to a close, Griffith surprised his public by serving up a sympathetic portrait of one poverty-stricken family barely managing amid the rubble (each eating one potato a day) in *Isn't Life Wonderful?* (1924).

France's seminal genius, Abel Gance, whose *Napoleon* (1927) made war part of an epic adventure, also changed his tune after the Big War. His *J'accuse* (1937) details the struggles of a World War I veteran whose peacetime invention is usurped by his country's military for lethal purposes. Enraged, the inventor calls up an army of dead veterans to protest for peace. Since those early days, the pacifist cinema has come to set its celluloid sights on everything from war itself to specific wars, kinds of warfare, the political war machine, the military, and even the character of warriors. The results have been just as stirring as those of any hawkish homage ever made.

MILESTONE'S MILESTONE

It's hard to describe the true excellence of *All Quiet on the Western Front* (1930). Let it suffice to say that although this movie was made during the infancy of talkies (in fact, it was started as a silent and only became a talkie during production), it packs the kind of punch that could have been packaged in 1950 or indeed 1990. This film, which is timeless in its power and style, describes the passage of an idealistic, butterfly-collecting young German soldier, Paul Baumer (Lew Ayers), and his schoolmates from idealism to disillusionment as they fight the French. The brutality and beauty of what the boys go through is heartbreaking (great dialogue and acting)

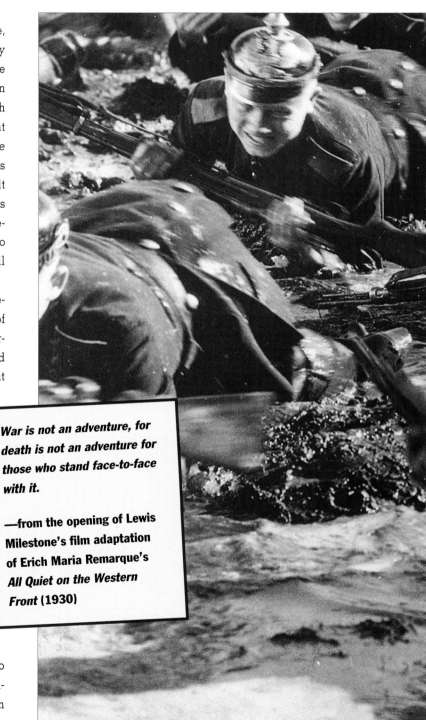

War is not an adventure, for death is not an adventure for those who stand face-to-face with it.

—from the opening of Lewis Milestone's film adaptation of Erich Maria Remarque's *All Quiet on the Western Front* (1930)

and horrifying (special effects that can make the most jaded audience squirm)—and consequently unforgettable.

Erich Maria Remarque, the author of the novel on which the movie was based, had served at the Western Front at the age of eighteen and was wounded several times. He called his novel "neither an accusation nor a confession"; he was just telling it like it was. Published in Germany in 1929 as *Im Westen nichts neues* (Nothing New in the West), the novel aroused considerable controversy. Irate nationalists accused Remarque of everything from having been too young to have fought in the war to being a French Jew to having merely edited the war diary of a dead friend to having first written a nationalistic, pro-war story and only changing his message to pacifism when the original didn't sell.

Nevertheless, his masterpiece was appreciated by many and almost immediately snapped up by equally misguided American publishers, who hyped the book as high adventure:

The most gripping novel in years. A drama of youth in a world aflame—of seven schoolboys whose only knowledge of life was limited to death, but whose short careers were packed with the adventure of a hundred years. Whose dreams, ideals, hopes, ambitions have been retold by a master of human analysis and words!!!

The young soldier Paul (Lew Ayers) learns the cost of blind patriotism as he crawls through the mud toward the French army in Lewis Milestone's All Quiet on the Western Front **(1930).**

A recently recovered Paul (Lew Ayers) hollowly tries to reassure a boneyard-bound comrade in **All Quiet on the Western Front (1930).**

Snappy copy like that sold seven million copies in the States, which convinced Hollywood that the novel was ripe for film adaptation. "Uncle" Carl Laemmle of Universal Studios bought the rights. Herbert Brenon, the director of *Beau Geste* (1927), was slated to direct for a $125,000 fee, but thirty-three-year-old Lewis Milestone underbid him, asking only $5,000 a week for a minimum of ten weeks.

After sequestering himself on southern California's Catalina Island for ten weeks to adapt the script with veteran Broadway writers Maxwell Anderson, Del Andrews, and George Abbott, Milestone went to work. Production started on the anniversary of Armistice Day, with real German guns, real uniforms, former German officers drilling the twenty-seven soldiers in the cast (which included future director Fred Zinnemann), and American Legion extras serving as both German and French combatants.

Borrowing montage techniques from Russian directors like Sergei Eisenstein and Dziga Vertov (a legendary Russian documentarian and film theorist who, along with Eisenstein, pioneered montage techniques), Milestone choreographed his battle scenes (which were filmed on 20 mined acres [8.1ha] of Laguna Beach, California, and shot silently using six cameras) to the

deadly rhythm of bombardment and his famous crane shot of massive casualties to the beat of machine-gun volleys. Death had never been so unblinkingly or powerfully portrayed (disembodied hands clutched barbed wire). The explosives technician who was working on another film at night got so jittery that he overdid his charges, knocking Milestone out in an explosion and causing the entire crew to wear steel German helmets for the duration of the filming.

War's effect on fighting men has rarely been shown so honestly. Pinned down in a crumbling bunker through days of shelling, some of Paul's young comrades start to lose their minds. Others squabble over the boots of a friend who has lost his legs. In the heat of another battle, a terrified Paul crawls into a foxhole and feigns death to escape certain destruction (a scene mirrored by actor John C. McGinley in Oliver Stone's *Platoon*, 1986). When a French poilu has the same idea and joins our hero in the hole, Paul stabs his adversary in the throat. But Milestone doesn't let this desperate act resolve too quickly. The Frenchman is not dead, only dying, and the now remorseful Paul is trapped in the hole face-to-face with this fellow human for the rest of the night. What transpires makes for one of the most uncomfortable war scenes ever recorded. (Ray Griffith, who played the dying soldier, did it for free, as a real throat problem made a career in the talkies impossible.)

This is not to say that the story was restricted by violence. Milestone brought the young stage director (and future film great) George Cukor to coach his actors in their dialogue scenes, and the care shows. Paul's relationship with the paternal Sergeant Katchinsky (the wonderful, broken-nosed actor Louis Wolheim) is touchingly real. His conversations and gripes with his buddies about the war seem uncannily candid and contemporary. Their one-night liaison with a group of starving French girls is frank and sexy. His scenes with his sick mother, played by Beryl Mercer, are saccharine-free. And throughout, Lew Ayers' nuanced, emotional performance is something you'd expect more from James Dean than an olden golden boy.

After $2 million and seventeen weeks of shooting and editing (with the added time, Milestone's fee came out to $10,000 more than his original competition), Milestone had almost 140 minutes of marvelous footage, but no ending. Remarque's book told nothing of its protagonist's unspecified demise. With Universal getting nervous about production running late, relief came in the ample form of the great Czech cinematographer Karl Freund. The soon-to-immigrate cameraman for such films as *Frankenstein* (1931) had struck up a friendship with Milestone. In response to Milestone's nagging question of how to kill off his hero, Freund responded, "It should be as simple as a butterfly." That it was, and just as exquisite (though it was Lewis Milestone's own hand that was framed in the famous shot, not Lew Ayers'). And the tag of Paul looking hauntingly back at the camera as his ghost image and those of soldiers in other countries' uniforms walk to an enormous graveyard is so powerful that Milestone admitted upon seeing the rushes that he "wanted to jump in there after them."

Like its literary inspiration, Milestone's *All Quiet on the Western Front* faced its share of flak. The Third Reich abhorred it. Propaganda minister Joseph Goebbels' brown-shirted goons picketed its run and released rats, snakes, and stink bombs inside the theaters playing the film. For some reason the French were incensed as well—censors refused a certificate for a French version for a full thirty-three years. But it is not an indictment of anything other than extreme nationalism and war. As Paul says upon revisiting the jingoistic professor who lured him into enlisting in the first place:

> I heard you in here reciting that same old stuff—making more Iron Men, more young heroes! You still think it's beautiful and sweet to die for your country, don't you? Well, we used to think you knew but the first bombardment taught us better. It's dirty and painful to die for your country. When it comes to dying for your country, it's better not to die at all.

THE BAD SIDE OF THE "GOOD WAR"

World War I's sudden end to gentlemanly clashes and entrenched beginning of mechanized slaughter was an easy target for commentary. Directors have taken aim at the Big War for decades—from Stanley Kubrick's career-launching *Paths of Glory* (1957), the antiwar story of a French commander named Dax (Kirk Douglas) who is punished with execution for refusing to obey the suicidal and self-glorifying commands of his superiors, to Peter Weir's career-launching collaboration with Mel Gibson, *Gallipoli* (1980), which tells of friendship and futility during the disastrous 1915 Allied assault on an Ottoman Turkish stronghold. World War II, however, was a different story.

In the mid-1930s, filmmaker Jean Renoir (son of impressionist painter Auguste Renoir), who had flown reconnaissance missions over Germany for France's C64 Squadron, smelled trouble brewing. With the help of French matinee idol Jean Gabin and former German director-turned-actor Erich Von Stroheim (whose 1923 silent *Foolish Wives* had convinced Renoir to take up a career in film...after he had watched it thirty-four times), Renoir turned out a plea for gentlemanly understanding between France and Germany: his masterful *La Grande Illusion* (1937).

Renoir knew all too well that European war was no longer cavalier or limited to gilded, dog-fighting, sword-brandishing daredevils. Before his last flight (almost the last one of his life) in World War I, he stoked himself with champagne, celebrating the birthday of a fellow flyer by skylarking with no preparation through low clouds to strafe a German-held village, "as lightheartedly as if we had been hunting rabbits." The Germans, however, had been prepared, and his captain's plane had crashed and burned in the blistering fire from below.

> *I saw this Jap machine-gunner squattin' on the ground. One of our Browning automatic riflemen had killed him. Took the top of his skull off. It rained all night. This Jap gunner didn't fall over for some reason. He was just sittin' upright in front of the machine gun. His arms were down at his sides. His eyes were wide open. It had rained all night and the rain had collected in his skull. We were just sittin' around on our helmets, waitin' to be relieved. I noticed this buddy of mine just flippin' chunks of coral into the skull about 3 feet [0.9m] away. Every time he'd get one in there, it'd splash. It reminded me of a child throwin' pebbles into a puddle. It was just so unreal. There was nothin' malicious in his actions. This was a just a mild-mannered kid who was now a twentieth-century savage.*
>
> —E.B. (Sledgehammer) Sledge, World War II marine, in Studs Terkel's *The Good War*, an oral history of World War II

> There was nothing on the beach [Omaha Beach] but dead bodies and the sand was red with blood.
>
> I remember they gave us a little vial of morphine to break and stick yourself in the arm with in case you got hit and were dying, it made dying easier. I don't think I had that morphine over one minute after I got on the beach. I gave it to another fellow. All these screaming things, mortars and artillery shells and all, you'd hear them whistling and you'd hit the dirt, well, when you hit the dirt every time you hit on top of another dead GI. There wasn't any such thing as digging a foxhole in the sand.
>
> —Lieutenant William H. Jones, 7th Battery, 467th Antiaircraft Artillery Battalion, in Russell Miller's *Nothing Less than Victory: The Oral History of D-Day*

Renoir's film, which was based largely on interviews with former P.O.W.s and writer Charles Spaak's remembrances, revealed the common humanity of German captors (especially the genteel, saber-scarred, crippled commandant, Captain Von Raufenstein—a part that Von Stroheim had merged from two characters in the original script) and their French captives at a château-turned-prison camp. The world loved it. Renoir's film won the Mussolini Cup at the 1937 Venice Film Festival (despite a ban by Italian censors). Even the Nazi press hailed it (though when they captured Paris, the Nazis confiscated all the copies they could find). But all this praise did not prevent the onset of World War II. And as the movie's title implied, trying to stop future wars was a less than realistic goal.

Seven years later, on June 6, 1944, participants in the D-Day invasion of Omaha Beach in Normandy, France, would come to understand this all too well. The D-Day invasion was the greatest amphibious military operation that the world had ever seen. The Allies put ashore 176,475 men, three thousand guns, fifteen hun-

dred tanks, and fifteen thousand other vehicles. Some eleven thousand ships were involved. More than ten thousand air sorties were flown to cover the landing troops. And there were 10,274 casualties on the first day alone, but that's a detail that the history books usually leave out and that the majority of films made during the war didn't spend much time on either. Even in the epic classic of the Normandy invasion, *The Longest Day* (1962), death is eclipsed by the razzle-dazzle of military planning and strategy—bloodshed takes a backseat to the scope of history.

Antiwar sentiment over the Second World War did not really filter in until well after the war was over, and some of this sentiment continued even into the 1990s. One of the latest examples was *A Midnight Clear* (1992), young director Keith Gordon's film adaptation of William Wharton's tale of an uneasy but tender (and fatally brief) Christmas truce between regular German army soldiers and American troops (all whiz kids from a reconnaissance intelligence group) in the Ardennes forest toward the end of the war in Europe.

One of the most original, most powerful, most politically correct, and most surprising antiwar movies was served up by macho Hollywood B-movie idol Cornel Wilde. *Beach Red* (1967) told a story of marines landing on and trying to hold an anonymous Japanese-occupied Pacific island—at a terrible cost. It turned out to be something of a sneak attack.

When *Beach Red* first got under way, it seemed so red-bloodedly American that Wilde got military assistance and approval

ABOVE: Gary Sinise has the crazy idea to signal for peace across enemy lines while guarding a wintry French château in Keith Gordon's antiwar flick, A Midnight Clear (1992). OPPOSITE: It will take more than a bandage to stop all the bleeding in actor-director Cornel Wilde's unblinking look at combat, Beach Red (1967).

from almost everyone. The Marine Corps, the Defense Department, and the American Legion jumped on board; even the Philippine army and navy were behind it. Wilde spent $1.8 million of United Artists' money (and came in under budget) in a forty-one-day shoot on the Philippine island of Luzon, 120 miles (193km) north of Manila (where filming persisted through four typhoons). He spurned makeup for his actors (except lots of blood) and made anyone playing a soldier wear 42 pounds (19kg) of equipment on the beach at all times. Within the first two days the makeup man, the props man, and the special effects man stalked off the set. Something not quite traditional was going on here.

Using almost no stock battle footage, Wilde was adapting Peter Bowman's 1945 novel to show how "War Is Hell" for everybody—not just the Allies. And this was the rub. Spending almost as much time filming the Japanese perspective as the American, he crafted a message with few ethnic or racial stereotypes and included equal-time flashback footage (in almost surreal colors) during which the minds of both Japanese and American soldiers could wander to their families. This honesty gives the

film's climax, a deadly and poignant face-to-face encounter between two supposed enemies (this time in separate foxholes), an impact that is almost equal to the foxhole scene in *All Quiet on the Western Front*.

Wilde pulled no punches in taking the glamour out of dying, as well as showing what it meant to men on both sides. Troops (or stuntmen and dummies) were blown up into the air like clods of dirt. One marine had his arm blown off by shrapnel. Hundreds of extra dialogue audio tracks were shot and added to an inter-woven barrage of screams, explosions, planes, rustling grass, and ragged breathing.

The result? Some condemned Wilde for a sadistic streak because he dwelt on violence. Others hailed his honesty. *The Los Angeles Herald Examiner* said that *Beach Red* came across the screen with "such force that it left the viewer shell-shocked. It is a paralyzing masterpiece." *Playboy* magazine went so far as to say, "This, by God, must be how it is to fight." The Defense Department, however, asked to have the marines' assistance deleted from the film's credits.

THE REEL THING

Beach Red *(1967)* may have been real compared with many war movies, but some movies about war were absolutely real (except for the bits of docudrama and propaganda). "Documentaries" are as important a part of any war-film fan's feast as fictional films. To help you make sure that your diet of bullets, blasts, and ballyhoo is balanced by bare facts, front-line footage, and in-depth interviews (along with a soupçon of propaganda from all sides), here is a short list of some of the war documentaries that you won't want to miss. Check the shelves of your favorite video store and the schedule for your local public television channel.

TRIUMPH OF THE WILL *(1935)*—

In 1934, the Nazi party rally rolled into Nuremberg, Germany (where the war-crimes trials were later held). The plucky, brilliant filmmaker Leni Riefenstahl, who was lucky enough to be in the Führer's good graces, turned it into a Wagnerian visual rhapsody. Even though Joseph Goebbels was extremely peeved that his Ministry of Propaganda didn't get to do it, he and everyone else later conceded that Riefenstahl's movie was the most stirring piece of propaganda ever made. The images are grand, the camera work is phenomenal, Hitler is the star, and the message (without mentioning anti-Semitism) is ugly and brutish despite all its optimism.

Leni Reinfenstahl's masterpiece of patrotic propaganda, Triumph of the Will *(1935), is guaranteed to stir the heart—until you remember that it was made for Hitler.*

THE SPANISH EARTH *(1937)*—With

Dutch documentarian Joris Ivens at the camera, Virgil Thompson and Marc Blitzstein composing music, and Ernest Hemingway narrating his own text, this look at the Spanish Civil War is one class act.

OLYMPIA *(1938)*—Sports buffs won't want to miss

this sumptuous look at the 1936 Olympic games in Berlin. No element of the body beautiful (even black American track legend Jesse Owens') escaped Riefenstahl's all-seeing eye. The mythic Greek frame for the movie, the revolutionary camera techniques, the painful close-ups of exhausted marathoners, and the men's diving, with its birdlike imagery, all make this the best sports film ever (even if the sponsors left something to be desired).

THE 400 MILLION *(1939)*—Ivens strikes

gold once again with this chronicle of China's little-publicized war against an invading Japan (and the heroic Chinese Communists), written by Hollywood screenwriter Dudley Nichols and narrated by the great actor Fredric March.

LONDON CAN TAKE IT *(1940)*, LISTEN TO BRITAIN *(1942)*, and FIRES WERE STARTED *(1943)*—Only

the Brits would have had the guts and eccentricity to give the humorously minded surrealist painter and poet Humphrey Jennings the job of chronicling their people's pluck in the face of war or of rallying around the brigades of citizen firefighters who waged a constant war with the Nazis' incendiary bombs. Mozart's music is mixed with the symphony of sounds coming from England's defense industries

WHY WE FIGHT *(1942–1945)*—Frank Capra

was at the helm for this seven-part series of U.S. WWII propaganda-information films. Capra and directors Anthony Veiller and Anatole Litvak had surprisingly free rein. In fact when Capra asked Chief of Staff General George C. Marshall what to do if he couldn't figure out U.S. policy on a topic, the general replied, "In those cases, make your own best estimate and see if they don't agree with you later." Though decidedly nationalistic (even paranoiac in the last episode), these thoughtful films are a must for getting the big historical picture. The individual films that make up the series are Prelude to War *(1942)*, The Nazi Strike *(1943)*, Divide and Conquer *(1943)*, The Battle of Britain *(1943)*, The Battle of Russia *(1943)*, The Battle of China *(1944)*, and War Comes to America *(1945)*.

THE MEMPHIS BELLE *(1944)*—What

was it like to fly inside the legendary B-17 "Flying Fortress"? William Wyler's forty-two minutes of rare color footage from WWII salutes the crew of one plane and the rigors and dangers they faced on their twenty-fifth and final bombing mission.

A taste of life under Vichy rule, Marcel Ophuls' epic of occupation, The Sorrow and the Pity (1969), is one of the best documentaries ever made.

THE NEGRO SOLDIER (1944)—Made

under Capra's supervision, this film by Stuart Heisler is a tribute to the African-American fighting man in World War II. (It doesn't mention that the U.S. armed forces were racially segregated during the war, but its impact may have hastened President Harry Truman's postwar integration of the armed forces.)

THE BATTLE OF SAN PIETRO (1945)—John Huston crafted this unglam-

orized documentation of American forces on a campaign through southern Italy. The film pulls no punches when it comes to the heavy casualties incurred in the fighting or the sometimes less than heroic welcomes that the Allies received when rolling into Italian towns and villages. Originally finished at forty minutes, the military initially edited the film down to a less harsh, thirty-minute version (which deletes scenes like the ones where soldiers ply terrified bambinos with candy to get them to smile appropriately for the cameras) for distribution. Both are now in circulation.

LET THERE BE LIGHT (1946)—

Huston's greatest contribution to the documentary genre is this unflinching portrait of shell-shocked veterans in a Long Island, New York, hospital after the war. Even though the message was that with psychotherapy there was help for these suffering soldiers, the military didn't jibe with the view that men could come back from combat anything but better for the experience. The film was locked away for three decades.

NIGHT AND FOG (1955)—French director

Alain Resnais's fast-moving, compelling, eerie, gruesome, unwatchable, unstoppable, gripping, and gritty revisitation of the death camp at Auschwitz-Birkenau. Combining ghostly footage of the unhallowed ground today with horrific images taken by the Nazis and by the camp's liberators and asking

questions, questions, questions of its viewers, this is one of the most powerful antiwar statements ever made.

THE SORROW AND THE PITY

(1969)—Marcel Ophuls' monumental four-and-a-half-hour examination of a town (Clermont-Ferrand) under the Nazi Vichy occupation was assembled from wartime newsreel footage and more than sixty hours of interviews with both collaborators and freedom fighters. What is the humanity of evil? What was one of Woody Allen's favorite films in Annie Hall (1977)? Watch and find out.

HEARTS AND MINDS (1975)—

There's no question that the slant here is against American involvement in Vietnam, but Peter Davis made the war's face so compellingly human that he was given an Academy Award anyway. Packed full of front-line (including North Vietnamese) and back-home footage, this movie provides revealing interviews with grieving, uncomprehending Vietnamese civilians ("First they bomb us. Then they come and photograph it all"); gung-ho American ex-P.O.W.s ("If it wasn't for the people, [Vietnam] would be very pretty"); emotionally and physically scarred veterans ("I think of my children now, and what I did"); policy makers like William Fulbright, Clark Clifford, George McGovern, and Stuart Rostrow (who sued for the film's censure once he saw how bad he looked in it); an eloquent Daniel Ellsberg ("It's a tribute to the American public that its leaders knew they had to be lied to. It's not a tribute that is was so easy to be lied to"); and a pontificating General Westmoreland ("The Oriental doesn't put the same high price on life as does the Westerner")—all to underscore the unintentional futility of President Lyndon Johnson's prediction that "the ultimate victory [in Vietnam] will depend on the hearts and minds of the people who actually live there."

THE LIFE AND TIMES OF ROSIE THE RIVETER (1980)—Connie

Field takes a long-overdue look at the incredible commitment (and incredible change) American women made when they took over much of the light industry to supply the troops in WWII. She also notes the racist and otherwise raw deal they got for all their efforts.

SHOAH (1985)—The last word on how the Holocaust

could have happened (if it isn't with God) is contained in French filmmaker Claude Lanzmann's almost nine-and-a-half-hour look at the death camps of the Nazis, the people who suffered them, and the people who ran them. With an ever-mounting arsenal of evidence, it makes the case that this genocide was no anomaly but a deliberate outgrowth of historic practices and that it was much more widely known among the German people than supposed.

UP THE MILITARY WITH SCALPEL AND CAMERA

Some films just don't want to respect anything, least of all the military. From Abbott and Costello's slapstick *Buck Privates* (1941) and John Ford's more realistic *Mister Roberts* (1955) to Mike Nichols' intellectual *Catch-22* (1970), Goldie Hawn's pampered *Private Benjamin* (1980), Ivan Reitman's lunatic *Stripes* (1981), and Damon Wayans' sadistic *Major Payne* (1995), directors and actors have been taking comedic potshots at the military mind-set. Bad boy Robin Williams' tour de force tirade as fast-talking armed forces disc-jockey Adrian Cronauer in Barry Levinson's *Good Morning, Vietnam* (1988) was the kind of comment on institutionalized insanity that might never have come along had it not been for another bad boy named Robert Altman and the troublemakers of *MASH* (1969).

MASH was the epitome of irreverence. In 1969 writer Ring Lardner Jr. was asked by a New York publisher to read the galleys and write the dust-jacket copy for a book by Richard Hornberger, a Massachusetts doctor who had served in the Korean

War and written a scathing comedy about the 4,077th Mobile Army Surgical Hospital that he had been a part of.

Lardner adapted Hornberger's story of surgeons operating on mangled soldiers 3 miles (4.8km) from the front and 6,718.5 miles (10,812.1km) from New York's Presbyterian Hospital. The two leads, Hawkeye Pierce and Trapper John McIntyre, two hedonistic heels who treated women almost purely as sex objects, were rebellious insubordinates who flouted military authority, devotees of drinking and golf—and excellent surgeons. The only shot fired in the whole script was from a referee's gun during an army football game. Most of the script was slice-of-life vignettes. Needless to say, Hollywood didn't quite know what to do with it.

Twentieth Century Fox's Richard Zanuck talked of moving the whole story into Vietnam with Jack Lemmon and Walter Matthau as the leads. Lardner quickly countered, saying that because of the

Is nothing sacred? No, it's not the Last Supper, just the farewell supper for a suicidal, homophobic dentist (John Schuck), as orchestrated by Hawkeye Pierce (Donald Sutherland) and Trapper John (Elliot Gould) in Robert Altman's irreverent MASH (1969).

football game the leads would need to be younger men in their prime. The men that Lardner and producer Ingo Preminger (Otto's brother) had in mind were rising stars Donald Sutherland and Elliot Gould, who were definitely interested. The problem was, no big-name directors were interested. Fifteen notables turned the vignette-riddled project down. Then Robert Altman came along.

In 1969 Robert Altman was a successful television director (of shows like *Bonanza*) who was trying to make the move to the big screen. He had been fired by Jack Warner from his first big feature, *Countdown* (1968), for having more than one person talking onscreen at the same time, and his small film, *That Cold Day in the Park* (1968), had won critical praise but was a little too arty to get much Hollywood attention. He wanted a shot at something juicy and the *MASH* script, he said, was made for him (although he largely obliterated the screenplay through improvisation). Having piloted a B-24 in World War II, he had a few bones to pick with the military himself.

While Altman didn't have much say in the "star" casting (he had wanted *Bonanza*'s Dan Blocker in one of the leads), he was able to import many supporting and background "improvisers" from places such as San Francisco's American Theater Ensemble. In the end, fourteen of the twenty-eight speaking roles were filled by actors making their screen debuts (Frankie Avalon turned down the role of Radar O'Reilly), and the ensemble (which featured such later luminaries as René Auberjonois, Michael Murphy, and Bud Cort) became a talent pool that Altman would dip into again and again throughout his career.

Pitted against the script's dynamic duo (Hawkeye and Trapper) were a pious religious nut, Major Frank Burns (Robert Duvall), and his lover, a sexually repressed chief nurse known as "Hot-Lips" Houlihan (Sally Kellerman). The scene in which Hot-Lips gets her nickname is one of the most outrageously funny scenes that ever employed a microphone.

Soon after Altman joined the team, production began on the Fox Ranch in the Santa Monica Mountains over Malibu (where one of the thirty vintage jeeps used in the film still stands). The atmosphere there was a combination of film set, summer camp, and commune for the three hundred actors, extras, and crew members. Altman, like the characters in his film, was extremely unconventional. After shooting was finished each day, he would show the dailies to anyone who was interested (something that simply was not done). These nightly viewings were great parties, and everyone would get blotto as one big happy family. His rehearsals and shots were continually improvised (that dropped body in the opening shot is a blunder that added a touch of realism). Dialogue was always overlapping. Almost every scene was shot using a Number 3 fog filter—"for a funky, dirty look"—and a zoom lens so that the director could take close-ups without the actors knowing. Since no one knew when the camera might zoom in, every actor had to be acting all the time. He announced to the cast that the best thing would be if they all won the Oscar for best supporting actor. This was fine for the improvisers, but for Gould and Sutherland it took a

while to get into the lack of hierarchy and the relaxed swing of things. For Kellerman:

> *It was one of the first times I let go and said, "I'll take chances. I'm going to be as big as it calls for in the part. It'll probably be the end of my career, but I'm going to enjoy the experience."* That's what Bob Altman inspires in you—the enjoyment.

The fun paid off. *MASH* is a totally engrossing lunatic microcosm of dire necessity and adolescent anarchy. The military's authority is subverted at every turn and through any means possible, including druggings and blackmail. Each oddball character is as convincing as he or she is improbable. And Altman extends the iconoclasm of Lardner's script and Hornberger's story into the editing room—scene endings are mixed, matched, and reshuffled (the money-counting scene after the football game was originally shot after a poker game that was edited out). A blanket of continual background sounds, off-screen dialogue, and camp P.A. system announcements are added to the sound mix in a pioneering move that extends the movie's reality beyond the camera frame. And the screenplay ending, which has Hawkeye and Trapper returning home to their stateside lives, was completely ditched when Altman's friend John T. Kelly suggested that the director instead use the ubiquitous P.A. system to reprise the cast—"Tonight's movie has been *MASH*, starring...." From beginning to end, the movie is nonstop rule-breaking.

Altman completed the film three days under his ten-week schedule—even after spending an entire week filming the *MASH* game with gridiron stars like Fran Tarkenton, John Meyers, and Nolan "Super Gnat" Smith. It was in the can and edited for $500,000 under budget. The army and the air force banned it at first, but later relented when they saw how good it was. The MPAA threatened an X rating for the spicy script. Altman soothed them by promising to cut any scenes they didn't like. And when Fox brass—who had been occupied during production with colossal projects like *Tora! Tora! Tora!* (1969) and *Hello, Dolly!* (1969)—saw it, they wanted a complete re-edit. Producer Preminger persuaded them to preview it to an audience in San Francisco. The audience loved it, so Fox executives decided that they loved it, too. *MASH* launched the careers of one of the best directors in Hollywood and of numerous actors, picked up the International Grand Prix at Cannes that year, and made more than thirteen times its $3 million cost in video rentals.

One last fun fact revolves around the movie's theme song, "Suicide Is Painless." When Altman's teenage son, Mike, who wrote the song, was asked by Preminger what payment he desired for his iconoclastic creativity, Mike said that all he wanted was a new guitar. The producer, wiser in ways financial, managed to convince him that royalties on a catchy tune like this one might be a better idea. With the popularity of the song and its long life on the subsequent television series, Robert Altman likes to complain that his son made more money on *MASH* than he ever did.

A MIRACLE OF MOMENTS

Sometimes the best way to politicize an issue is to humanize it. Francis Ford Coppola called his sprawling, magnificent *Apocalypse Now* (1979) "high, epic adventure." As high-minded and epic as it was, it was also so surreally impersonal that putting yourself in its character's shoes was a challenge many viewers weren't up to. Michael Cimino's tenderly filmed *The Deer Hunter* (1979) told of the war's impact on a circle of friends and an American way of life through harrowing archetypal events. However, a year before either of these legendary Vietnam films hit the screens, Hal Ashby's *Coming Home* (1978) focused on the changes wrought by war using a more intimate lens.

When two men come home from the Vietnam War, one is physically whole yet mentally shattered and the other is physically broken but mentally sound. One woman is torn between them—the first man is her husband; the second is the paralyzed soldier she has nursed, befriended, and fallen in love with. Sounds like a soap opera? Not the way Jane Fonda, Jon Voight, and Bruce Dern do it, and not to a running soundtrack of the very best rock from the 1960s and 1970s.

Jon Voight and Jane Fonda get ready to make love not war (in one of the most sensual love scenes ever recorded) in Hal Ashby's Coming Home (1978).

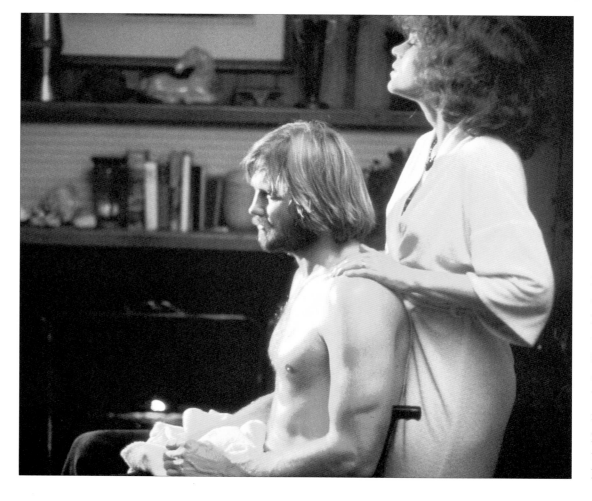

Easy Rider (1969) had broken several major movie rules and in the process had made the old formulas for hit films a little less ironclad. In the mid-1970s, studios were willing to take a chance; consequently, writers had more freedom. In 1973, Nancy Dowd had written a script about a Vietnam-era love triangle called *Buffalo Ghost*. Los Angeles–based antiwar activist Bruce Gilbert liked the premise and wanted to try his hand as a producer. He had cofounded a progressive, cooperative nursery called Blue Fairy Land, where Jane Fonda had enrolled her daughter, Vanessa. Both Fonda and Gilbert were also involved with the Indochina Peace Campaign run by Tom Hayden (Fonda's then-husband). Fonda and Gilbert started talking about "Peace Campaign Productions" and a film they might do on the war. With Jane's movie-star clout post-*Klute* (1971), this untouchable subject just might be touchable...eventually (even though her antiwar activities had earned her the nickname Hanoi Jane).

They brought in veteran script doctor Waldo Salt (*Midnight Cowboy*, 1969, and *Serpico*, 1974) to rewrite Dowd's story into a more workable script. Script doctor number two, Robert C. Jones, then polished Salt's 220-page rewrite. The result—five years later—was a story about Sally Hyde, a cheerful, faithful, conservative American marine wife who volunteers at the local veteran's hospital while her gung-ho husband, Bob, goes in country. At the hospital, she meets Luke Martin, a former high school football hero whom she used to cheerlead for, now a paraplegic vet whose anger and militancy against the war stirs her political consciousness and whose passionate humanity awakens her sleeping sexuality. Kapow! Love story and political message in one.

The studios, as it turned out, were interested in almost any Fonda vehicle. John Schlesinger (*Midnight Cowboy*), who was slated to direct, brought in his and Salt's old chum, the headstrong young actor Jon Voight for the part of the husband, Bob. Luke was to be played by Jack Nicholson...they hoped. But Nicholson demurred and though both Al Pacino and Sylvester Stallone were considered for the part, Voight's lobbying won the role, with Bruce Dern stepping in to play Bob. In the meantime, Schlesinger had withdrawn because he thought that his British sensibility made him unfit to lens such an American story. Hal Ashby, whose films like *The Last Detail* (1973) focused on small casts and intimate relationships, was a logical replacement.

The movie made by Ashby from Salt and Jones' script (the cast was given credit for 80 percent of the dialogue) is a miracle of small moments following the struggles of the three characters. And it never hits a didactic note. Each moment is well honed and emotionally charged: Sally's first small steps to independence and self-discovery; her first encounter with Luke, when she upsets his urine bag when he careens into her on a hospital corridor; Luke's chaining himself and his wheelchair to the gates of a local marine base; the tragic plight of a disturbed young veteran (Robert Carradine) who is her best friend's little brother; the first time she invites Luke over for dinner; the first time she sleeps with him; Bob's bewildered and boozy return and discovery of Sally's relationship with Luke; the resolution that awaits them all; Luke's attempt to come to terms with his feelings about the war while talking with a curious group of high school students. This film is crafted with an honesty and a simplicity that is deeply moving and, for that reason, deeply accusatory of the war in Vietnam.

One of the most moving moments is the love scene between Sally and Luke, which would almost be too intimate to watch if it weren't for its integrity. In five weeks of preparation for life in a wheelchair (during which he learned to play wheelchair basketball with the national champions, the Long Beach Raiders), Voight nearly doubled the size of his biceps, triceps, and back muscles. He is a believable paraplegic and buffed to boot. During his six weeks of living and filming with fifty paraplegic vets at the Downey, California, Veterans' Hospital, he barraged his new friends and teachers with questions on sex and every other aspect of their lives. He discovered the importance of their cultivated skill of oral sexual virtuosity.

Ashby, a veteran of near-explicit filmmaking because of his work on *Shampoo* (1975), put his experience and Voight's newly acquired knowledge to use in the thousands of feet of love scenes that he shot with Voight, Fonda, and the body double who took over the more revealing scenes for Jane. The love scenes added up to six hours of material (including explicit dialogue that never made it into the film); at the first dailies, Jane was less than thrilled: "Hal," she said, "this is just too graphic." A cut here and a cut there, and 6,000 feet (1,829m) was whittled down to 1,000 feet (305m), resulting in one of the hottest scenes in film history, let alone from any war film.

THIS IS THE WAY THE WORLD ENDS

Even at the end of the twentieth century, in our somewhat enlightened post–Cold War era, wars still rage. The Middle East is, as always, a battle zone (though an uneasy peace may be in sight). The former Yugoslavia is a wasteland of civil strife and "ethnic cleansing." Somalia and Rowanda bleed continually. But beyond the taking of Grenada (which didn't excite too many heroic scripts) and the Gulf War (which was so heavily televised that a film wasn't really necessary), the war that has really whet Hollywood's appetite when it comes to filmmaking is the Big One—the potential nuclear holocaust of World War III. Having tired of examining the horrors of nuclear war's aftermath with such films as *Testament* (1983) and *The Day After* (1983), Tinseltown took its newfound love for submarines (*The Hunt for Red October*, 1990) and put it to use in what could have been a war-thriller rehash of *Failsafe* (1964) or *The Bedford Incident* (1965). Ironically, what they came up with is a thoughtful and pulverizingly exciting movie.

Crimson Tide (1995) not only examines a military unit (a nuclear submarine crew) on the brink of launching Armageddon, but also examines the personalities of two diametrically opposed warriors who could control it—the experienced old-school soldier who follows his orders to the letter and the new-school soldier who thinks in more global terms. The situation is simple: a volatile Russian nationalist leader in the strife-torn former U.S.S.R. seizes control of a nuclear missile base and threatens to bomb the United States if the United Nations doesn't butt out of his grab for power. This sets off the biggest arms showdown since the Cuban missile crisis.

The crew of the USS *Alabama*, with possession of more firepower than any place on the face of the earth, waits to see if a preemptive strike will be necessary. Their captain is the keenly intelligent, hard-edged hawk Frank Ramsey (Gene Hackman making $4 million), and their new executive officer is the intellectual, cool-headed dove (or close to it) Ron Hunter (Denzel Washington making $7 million). While being chased by a Russian Akula Class hunter-killer submarine, the *Alabama* receives a partial message that looks like the code for commitment to attack. With time for an effective strike running out and the survival of the whole world at stake, Ramsey and Hunter (and their factions) duke it out (at times, literally) for control of the craft.

Duking it out was what making this picture was all about. When it came to the lead roles, there were many battles, and Hackman and Washington weren't the only contenders. Warren Beatty–Val Kilmer and Al Pacino–Andy Garcia combinations were also considered, but they were mercifully dismissed.

Michael Schiffer had written a macho thinking man's script (which he referred to as "*12 Angry Men* [1957] on a submarine")

AND YOU THOUGHT *MASH* WAS WEIRD—WAY-OUT WAR FILMS

Every now and then, a director uses the war film motif to express something that goes way beyond the battlefield. The following is a list of war movies that definitely operate on a higher and, in some cases, more cosmic plane.

TO BE OR NOT TO BE (1942)—
Jack Benny and Carole Lombard head up a zany troupe of Polish actors who happen to be playing Warsaw when the Nazis take it. They soon find themselves ditching Shakespeare for espionage.

THE MOUSE THAT ROARED
(1959)—The tiny European country of Grand Fenwick, finding itself broke, decides to declare war on the United States in order to rake in war reparations when they lose. Peter Sellers does his multicharacter best—he plays Fenwick's commander in chief, prime minister, and grand duchess.

THE MANCHURIAN CANDIDATE (1962)—John Frankenheimer
serves up a cold dish of Cold War paranoia in this wild tale of Korean vet Lawrence Harvey, who comes back to Washington, brainwashed, to assassinate the president. Only brainwashed buddy Frank Sinatra can possibly stop the hideous plot.

DR. STRANGELOVE, OR: HOW I LEARNED TO STOP WORRYING AND LOVE THE BOMB (1963)—Peter Sellers does his
multiple personality thing again—playing an unflappable British officer, an American president, and the mad scientist (and Henry Kissinger look-alike) of the title—in this brilliant Stanley Kubrick flick spoofing Cold War paranoia.

THE NIGHT OF THE GENERALS (1966)—Peter O'Toole plays a
fair-haired Nazi boy–cum–wonder general, but military policeman Omar Sharif knows that he is also a madman killer who has spent part of his wartime life killing prostitutes for kicks. Can he crack the general's ironclad reputation, or is the serial killer too crafty to be caught?

KING OF HEARTS (1966)—French
director Philippe de Broca's tender antiwar statement features Alan Bates as a WWI Scottish soldier who stumbles onto a French town that is deserted, except for the residents of the local loony bin.

HOW I WON THE WAR (1967)—
Michael Crawford (Phantom of the Opera) and John Lennon costar in this story, directed by Richard Lester (A Hard Day's Night), about a twit of a British officer whose aim is to set up a cricket field in the North African desert during WWII.

REFLECTIONS IN A GOLDEN EYE (1967)—With John Huston
directing, Elizabeth Taylor, Marlon Brando, Brian Keith, and Julie Harris team up to deliver writer Carson McCullers' twisted view of fear, loathing, and repressed (and flagrant) sexuality at a southern military base.

OH, WHAT A LOVELY WAR
(1969)—Yes, it's Sir Richard Attenboro's all-dancing, all-singing, hallucinogenic lark about European war-mongering, featuring such sensational musical stars as Laurence Olivier, John Gielgud, Dirk Bogarde, Susannah York, Vanessa Redgrave, Michael Redgrave, and Jane Seymour. War movies don't get much more Britishly eccentric than when the dead are tallied on a giant cricket scoreboard.

SLAUGHTERHOUSE FIVE
(1972)—Kurt Vonnegut's time-tripping WWII GI, Billy Pilgrim (Michael Sacks), bops from Dresden to the planet Tralfamador, where his connubial activities with sex-kitten Montana Wildhack (Valerie Perrine) are subject to alien scrutiny.

APOCALYPSE NOW (1979)—Joseph
Conrad's novel of African odyssey, The Heart of Darkness, meets Francis Ford Coppola's vision of the insanity of the American war in Vietnam, resulting in one of the best and weirdest movies ever made. Martin Sheen (narrator assassin), Marlon Brando (crazed, godlike, renegade commander and blimp-sized target), Robert Duvall (indestructible war lover who cranks Wagner during air strikes), Dennis Hopper (gonzo acolyte photographer), Frederic Forrest (New Orleans saucier turned soldier), Sam Bottoms (California surfer turned soldier), and Larry Fishburne (street punk turned soldier) play the almost mythic characters that populate this descent into the underworld.

LION OF THE DESERT

(1979)—Libyan leader and terrorist Mu'ammar Qaddafi footed much of the bill for this homage to Omar Mukhtar, the Bedouin guerrilla leader who stopped Italian raids in Libya from 1911 to 1931. Anthony Quinn, Oliver Reed, Rod Steiger, and John Gielgud star.

MEPHISTO

(1981)—Klaus Maria Brandauer plays a German actor whose specialty is playing Mephistopheles in Goethe's Faust, but whose bread is now buttered by the real devil leading the Third Reich. What price success? Watch and find out through one of the finest screen performances ever.

MERRY CHRISTMAS, MR. LAWRENCE

(1983)—David Bowie and Tom Conti star in a movie about British POWs in a Japanese concentration camp run by a commandant (Ryuichi Sakamoto) with a crush on the rocker in uniform. Thanks to Japanese director Nagisa Oshima, it actually comes off quite well (even the flashbacks of Bowie betraying his hunchbacked little clarion-voiced brother).

THE KEEP

(1983)—It had to happen. Nazi troops led by officers Scott Glenn and Gabriel Byrne occupy an ancient fortress high in the Carpathian Mountains only to discover that it was built to "keep something in," not to keep anyone out. Can the Third Reich tackle an evil even greater than itself?

BIRDY

(1985)—Matthew Modine is a shell-shocked Vietnam vet who thinks he's...that's right...a bird. And it's up to Nicolas Cage (and director Alan Parker) to bring him back to painful reality.

EMPIRE OF THE SUN

(1987)—Only Stephen Spielberg could have codirected this WWII boy's fantasy adventure set in a Japanese prison camp (with Frank Marshall and David Tomblin). Christian Bale stars as a kid whose world changes for better and worse after being forced to flee his home in Shanghai.

JACOB'S LADDER

(1990)—Is postman–Vietnam vet Tim Robbins seeing angels and demons on the streets of New York because of a horrible chemical experiment that the military perpetrated on his platoon, or is it something much stranger?

> *My film is not about Vietnam. It is Vietnam. The way we made it was very much the way we were in Vietnam. We were in the jungle, there were too many of us, and little by little we went insane.*
>
> **—Francis Ford Coppola on Apocalypse Now (1979)**

that focused on the personal struggles and moral fiber of two dedicated men. In early 1993, Schiffer had managed to wangle several Disney brass aboard the immense USS *Florida* out of Bangor, Washington, for a daylong cruise. He had also somehow managed to convince its 180-man crew to stage dramatic moments from his script, including a missile drill with countdown and launch, a fire drill, and an armed search of the ship to ferret out an unidentified security threat. Needless to say, this show-and-tell brought the dramatic possibilities home to the Disney executives.

Still, with all the moola that the $470 million–grossing, high-tech *Top Gun* (1986) director Tony Scott would need for this blockbuster, the studio wanted to make sure they had the best script Hollywood could provide. In swooped some top-gun screenwriters. Quentin Tarantino (*Reservoir Dogs*, 1992) did a few weeks of spiffing (for a mere $350,000), adding human touches like Denzel's Silver Surfer comic book moment. Steve Zallian (*Schind-ler's List*, 1994) made a few dialogue improvements. Bad boy Robert Towne (*Chinatown*, 1974) put in his two cents on the military history discussions between Hackman and Washington, as well as the final courtroom scene. And Hackman contributed his own last lines. Schiffer was unruffled: "These guys could punch up *Hamlet*," he said.

With the "software" taken care of, Scott practiced his own perfectionist talents with the "hardware." Dream Quest Images crafted the underwater exteriors using every contemporary trick they could muster, from computer graphics and digital image manipulation to motion control and high-speed photography of miniatures to matte paintings, detailed model construction, blue screen photography, animation, and optical compositing.

More than a decade earlier, similar technical challenges had been faced during the making of *Das Boot* ("The Boat," 1981), Germany's relentlessly harrowing portrait of an endangered World War II submarine crew and the film that brought submarine flicks back into vogue. Originally intended as a six-hour miniseries for German television, this film had much less to do with "evil Nazis" than with sailors and their fight for survival.

Out of forty thousand U-boat sailors forced into service of the Third Reich, thirty thousand had died at sea. German director Wolfgang Petersen wanted to honor these sailors with an adaptation of war correspondent Lothar-Gunther Buchheim's 1973 novel. Initially, this film was set drifting toward Americaniza-tion in the hands of director Don Siegel and actor Paul Newman. Fortunately, Petersen ultimately directed with an all-German cast, with Jurgen Prochnow giving a standout performance as the sub's heroic captain.

Das Boot was as up-close a portrait of fighting men under pressure (literally) as had ever been made. Like the original VII-C U-boat, Petersen's two 50-ton (45.3t) replicas (one for exteriors and one for interiors) were 150 feet (45.7m) long and only 8 feet (2.4m) wide

I have a fascination with people on the edge. There's a darkness and a weirdness to people whose lives revolve around violence or a violent occupation. I'm fascinated by men who want to go down in a shell under water for twenty-five days. It seems so alien to me.

—Tony Scott, on directing *Crimson Tide* (1995)

Dovish executive officer Denzel Washington (left) squares off with hawkish commanding officer Gene Hackman in the gripping submarine thriller Crimson Tide *(1995)*.

(35-, 18-, and 8-foot [10.6, 5.4, and 2.4m] models were used as well). Ironically, the plans for them came from Chicago's Museum of Science. The director refused to open up the space with removable walls; instead, he fitted his cameraman with a helmet, knee pads, and elbowpads, and sent him into the madness of men in motion with a handheld, gyroscope-balanced Arriflex camera. That motion was ensured by a 16-foot (4.8m) gimbal called "the Wippler," which could simulate a complete array of submarine movement.

During the fifteen-week shoot of *Crimson Tide*, two sound-stages at Culver Studios were ravaged, ransacked, and reconstructed over eight weeks to support the largest hydraulic gimbal ever created. The giant gimbal is what held the submarine set and enabled it to move a full 30 degrees from port to starboard or from bow to stern in six seconds. It also provided a quick stop that was severe enough to simulate the shake and chaos that follows a torpedo or depth-charge explosion.

That kind of realism created various challenges inside the craft. As Washington remembered:

When the platform was actually moving back and forth it was kind of fun...like an E-ride [at Disneyland]. But when it was tilted at a very steep angle and stationary, it was difficult to walk, let alone act.

The movement of the gimbal wasn't the only technical challenge faced by the cast. For the nightmarish bilge-bay flood scene, actors were immersed in the chill waters of the Culver City,

California, Municipal Pool for fourteen hours—trapped in a set contained in a perforated 54-ton (48.6t), 44-foot (13.4m) cargo container.

For Hackman, however, the challenges were more internal than external. The lingo of underwater sailors presented some difficulty for him. As he recalls:

The vocabulary was alien to most of us. It was hard to learn that dialogue because it has no frame of reference in your life. It took a lot of rehearsals to get the proper sense of it so that it looked and sounded like those commands were second nature to us.

Fortunately, he had expert help in mastering his masterful attitude, perfecting protocol, and using a vocabulary that regularly included such unusual terms as "baffles," "conn," "zero bubble," and "weps." No less than two retired commanding officers of the real-life USS *Alabama* served as technical advisers. Captain Mal Wright and Captain Skip Beard, respectively, made suggestions on the script and on the set.

Together, Scott, Schiffer (et al), Hackman, and Washington (with the help of a superb supporting cast—or is that "crew"?) created a perfect boy's night out: a tight thriller that examines exactly what is worth fighting for (including peace) and to what extreme. Though the outcome is a foregone conclusion, the superb story, performances, and special effects make this state-of-the-art stunner as persuasively realistic as any antiwar film ever shot. To get any more real, we would have to remind ourselves of what the grizzled Sam Fuller, hard-bitten director of such war films as *Steel Helmet* (1951) and *Fixed Bayonets* (1951), once said:

The only way to make a war film realistic is to have someone with a rifle stand behind the screen and shoot at the audience.

BEHIND ALLIED LINES

At ease! Now that you've been steeped in guts and glory, let's see how well you recognize the lines that made the great lines from the greatest war films of all time. If you can match up the words with the actors and movies examined here (and a few more thrown in to test you further), you may win a Purple Heart for courage and heroic acts above and beyond the duty of eye-strain and writer's cramp.

LINE

1. "Ain't much matter what happens tomorrow, 'cause we men, ain't we!"

2. "I don't want to be rehabilitated, readjusted, reconditioned or re-anything. And if you don't mind, I don't want to take my proper place in society, either. Does that make my position clear?"

3. "Rommel, you magnificent bastard, I read your book!"

4. "I'm a veget-Aryan."

5. "Gladiators don't make friends. If we're ever matched in the arena together, I'll have to kill you."

6. "Dear Frances: We just blew a bridge and took a farm-house. It was easy. Terribly easy."

7. "Stick around, Kenny. We're gonna choose up sides for a snowball fight."

8. "This is our war. We will carry it with us from one battle-ground to another. In the end, we will win. I hope we can rejoice in our victory....As for those beneath the wooden crosses we can only murmur, 'Thanks, pal, thanks.'"

9. "Fuckin' A."

10. "You are defeated but you have no shame."

11. "Use of officers for labor is expressly forbidden by the Geneva Convention."

12. "I stick my neck out for nobody."

13. "I don't know who said the flesh was weak; I find it very strong."

14. "If he's running with you, he's a South Korean. If he's running after you, he's North Korean."

15. "I don't pretend to like the idea of killing a bunch of people, but it's a case of dropping a bomb on them or their dropping a bomb on Ellen."

16. "What he did to Shakespeare, we are doing now to Poland."

ACTOR AND FILM

A: Denzel Washington, Glory (1989)

B: Woody Strode, Spartacus (1960)

C: John Ireland, A Walk in the Sun (1946)

D: George Murphy, Battleground (1949)

E: Burgess Meredith, The Story of G.I. Joe (1945)

F: Chuck Aspergren, The Deer Hunter (1979)

G: Sessue Hayakawa, The Bridge on the River Kwai (1957)

H: Alec Guinness, The Bridge on the River Kwai (1957)

I: Walter Pidgeon, Mrs. Miniver (1942)

J: Gene Evans, Steel Helmet (1951)

K: Van Johnson, Thirty Seconds Over Tokyo (1944)

L: Humphrey Bogart, To Have and Have Not (1943)

M: Martin Sheen, Apocalypse Now (1979)

N: Burt Lancaster, Run Silent, Run Deep (1958)

O: J. Carrol Nash, Sahara (1943)

P: John Wayne, The Sands of Iwo Jima (1949)

Q: Jack Webb, The Men (1950)

R: Jon Voight, Coming Home (1978)

S: George C. Scott, Patton (1970)

LINE	ACTOR AND FILM
17. "There's always someone else. That's the mistake the Germans make with the people they try to destroy. There will always be someone else."	T: Aldo Ray, The Green Berets *(1968)*
18. "I want what every guy who came here to spill his guts wants—for our country to love us as much as we loved it."	U: Everett McGill, Heartbreak Ridge *(1986)*
19. "Let no one here, no one aboard this boat, ever say we didn't have a captain."	V: Robert Mitchum, The Longest Day *(1962)*
	W: Charles Chaplin, The Great Dictator *(1940)*
20. "Are my eyes blind that I should fall on my knees to worship a maniac who had made of my country a concentration camp?... It's because of a man like him that God, my God, created hell."	X: Gary Cooper, Sergeant York *(1941)*
21. "That's war—trading real estate for men."	Y: Sylvester Stallone, Rambo: First Blood Part II *(1985)*
22. "I'm as much agin' killin' as ever, but when I heard them machine guns...well, them guns was killin' hundreds, maybe thousands, and there weren't nuthin' anybody could do to stop them guns. That's what I done."	Z: Theresa Wright, The Men *(1950)*
	AA: Richard Conte, A Walk in the Sun *(1946)*
23. "We all belong to this airplane. We're a single team. Each one of us has got to rely on every other man doing the right thing at the right time. Teamwork is all that counts."	BB: John Ridgeley, Air Force *(1943)*
	CC: Robert Taylor, Bataan *(1943)*
24. "It was a real choice mission and when it was over I would never want another."	DD: Lee Marvin, The Big Red One *(1980)*
25. Come on, suckers, come and get me. We're still here—we'll always be here—come and get it."	EE: John Wayne, Flying Tigers *(1942)*
26. "We don't murder, we kill."	FF: Sig Rauman, To Be or Not To Be *(1942)*
27. "He should have stayed in college where he came from, but he begged for a chance—begged for it like some kid asking to go to the circus."	GG: Matthew Modine, Full Metal Jacket *(1987)*
	HH: Alan Hale, God Is My Co-Pilot *(1945)*
28. "We run two types of stories here: grunts who gave half their salary to buy gooks toothbrushes and deodorants, winning hearts and minds; and combat actions that result in a kill, winning the war."	II: Courtney Vance, Hamburger Hill *(1987)*
	JJ: Lew Ayers, All Quiet on the Western Front *(1930)*
29. "Son, you're not up there alone. You have the greatest copilot in the world."	KK: Gregory Peck, MacArthur *(1977)*
	LL: Katherine Hepburn, The African Queen *(1951)*
30. "A soldier goes where he is told to go, fights where he is told to fight."	MM: Paulette Goddard, So Proudly We Hail *(1943)*
	NN: George Macready, Paths of Glory *(1957)*

31. "You ought to be sealed in a case labeled, 'Break open: only in case of war.'"

32. "Only two kinds of people are going to stay on that beach—those that are dead and those who are going to die."

33. "I shall return."

34. "I never dreamed that any mere physical experience could be so stimulating."

35. "If those little sweethearts won't face German bullets, they'll face French ones."

36. "I love this place at night. The stars. There's no right, no wrong in them. They're just there."

37. "Darling, if I hadn't known that you'd taken a German pilot single-handed, I'd say you were scared."

38. "A wonderful boy loved you, Jane. That doesn't happen to everyone."

39. "I'm not marrying a wheelchair. I'm marrying a man."

40. "Nobody dies."

41. Q: "Where's all this push-button war we've been hearing about?" A: "We're the push-buttons."

42. "Ever see a lightbulb burn out, how bright the filament is before it lets go? I think they call it 'Maximum Effort.'"

43. "It don't mean nuthin', not a thing."

44. "We live in the trenches and we fight. We try not to be killed—that's all."

45. "My backbone fractured in two places, mended with silver plates. Silver strut in my chin, also a silver kneecap...I owe all this wealth to the misfortune of war."

46. "I'm a marine! I'm gonna kill those bastards, I'm gonna shoot them, I'm gonna bayonet them, I'm gonna break their arms....That's what we're here for—to kill. The rest is just crap!"

47. "This isn't 'have a gimp over for dinner' night, is it?"

OO: *Humphrey Bogart,* Casablanca *(1942)*

PP: *Willem Dafoe,* Platoon *(1987)*

QQ: *Claudette Colbert,* Since You Went Away *(1944)*

RR: *Gregory Peck and Rip Torn,* Pork Chop Hill *(1959)*

SS: *Gary Merrill,* Twelve O'Clock High *(1949)*

TT: *Erich Von Stroheim,* Grand Illusion *(1937)*

UU: *Rip Torn,* Beach Red *(1967)*

Answers

1=A, 2=O, 3=S, 4=W, 5=B, 6=C, 7=D, 8=E, 9=F, 10=G,
11=H, 12=OO, 13=MM, 14=I, 15=K, 16=FF, 17=L, 18=V,
19=N, 20=O, 21=P, 22=X, 23=BB, 24=M, 25=CC, 26=DD,
27=EE, 28=GG, 29=HH, 30=T, 31=U, 32=V, 33=KK,
34=LL, 35=NN, 36=PP, 37=I, 38=OO, 39=Z, 40=AA,
41=RR, 42=SS, 43=II, 44=II, 45=TT, 46=UU, 47=R

BIBLIOGRAPHY

Anderson, Ted. "Paraplegic G.I. Relives War in Searing Scene." *Los Angeles Times*, 26 February 1950.

Ansen, David. "Spielberg's Obsession." *Newsweek*, 20 December 1995.

"Army o.k.s film on military. Navy bans it." *Los Angeles Times*, 20 August 1953.

Barna, Yon. *Eisenstein*. Bloomington, Ind.: Indiana University Press, 1973.

Bartel, Pauline. *The Complete "Gone With the Wind" Trivia Book*. Dallas: Taylor Publishers, 1989.

Battleground—facts for editorial reference. MGM Studios, 1949.

Beerman, Francis O. "The Real 'Blood and Guts' to Stand in for 20th's Patton." *Film and Television Daily*, 8 October 1968.

The Best Years of Our Lives—press campaign. RKO Radio Pictures, 1946.

"The Big Parade"—New York Museum of Modern Art interview with King Vidor. *New York Times*, 8 November 1925.

The Big Parade—souvenir program for premiere at Grauman's Egyptian Theater, 5 November 1925.

The Birth of a Nation—souvenir program. New York: Epoch Producing, 1915.

Bon Fante, Jordan, Sally Donnely, Richard Osling, and Michael Riley. "Cult of Death." *Time*, 15 March 1993.

Boyum, Joy G. "Looking Back at Vietnam." *Wall Street Journal*, 3 March 1975.

The Bridge on the River Kwai—press releases. Columbia Studios, 1956–1957.

Brown, Peter H. " 'Coming Home' Came Home with a Whole Lot of Loving." *Los Angeles Times*, 23 December 1979.

Buckley, Tom. "Cheers for Two after the Return of Napoleon." *New York Times*, 30 January 1981.

Cohn, Lawrence. "Filmmakers Survive Uphill Battle to Get 'Hill' Made." *Variety*, 25 August 1987.

Collins, Glenn. " 'Glory' Resurrects Its Black Heroes." *New York Times*, 26 March 1989.

Corliss, Richard. "Guns and Buttered Popcorn." *New Times*, 20 March 1978.

———. "The Man Behind the Monster." *Time*, 21 February 1994.

Crewe, Regina. " 'All Quiet on the Western Front' Epic War Film Mighty in Dramatic Power." *New York American*, 30 April 1930.

Crowther, Bosley. "The Birth of 'The Birth of a Nation.' " *New York Times Magazine*, 7 February 1965.

The Deer Hunter—program notes and press releases. Universal Pictures, 1978.

Delahanty, Thorton. "Over Three Selznick Hours in 'Since You Went Away.' " *New York Herald Tribune*, 20 February 1944.

"D.P. Children in New Movie." *Cue*, 13 March 1948.

Eisenstein, Sergei. "Battleship Potemkin." *The Nation*, 1927.

Emerson, Gloria. "Jon Voight: Making Peace with an Endless War." *Village Voice*, 20 February 1978.

Eyssell, G.S. Radio City Music Hall program for *Mrs. Miniver*. 23 July 1942.

Farmer, James. "The Making of Twelve O'Clock High." *Journal of the American Aviation Historical Society*, winter 1974.

Filipov, David. " 'Schindler's List' has weak debut in ignorant Moscow." *Press Telegram*, 17 September 1994.

"Film Is Reviving Legend of Lawrence of Arabia." *Los Angeles Mirror*, 26 August 1961.

"The Films of Erich Von Stroheim." Program notes from the Los Angeles County Museum of Art, 23 March 1985.

Flynn, Hazel. "Battleship Potemkin." *Beverly Hills Citizen*, 6 January 1960.

Foner, Eric, and John A. Garraty, eds. *The Reader's Companion to American History*. Boston: Houghton Mifflin, 1991.

"From Here to Eternity." *Colliers*, 7 August 1953.

Garfield, John. "The Role I Liked Best." *Saturday Evening Post*, 12 January 1946.

Gilliat, Penelope. "Work of a Master." *New Yorker*, 6 September 1976.

Gish, Lillian. "The Birth of a Nation." *Stage*, vol. 14, no. 4 (January 1937).

Glory—press packet. Tri-Star Pictures, 1989.

Gold, Mike. "Change the World." *Daily Worker*, 29 October 1938.

Grand Illusion. Los Angeles County Museum of Art screening, 23 March 1985.

Grant, James. "The Sub Genre Resurfaces." *Los Angeles Times Calendar*, 7 May 1995.

Griffith, D.W. *Sight and Sound*, vol. 16, no. 61 (spring 1947).

Grilli, Peter. "Kurosawa Directs a Cinematic 'Lear'." *New York Times*, 15 December 1985.

Grove, Martin A. "Fields Follow Up." *Hollywood Reporter*, 22 October 1989.

Hamburger Hill—press kit. 1987.

Hansard, David. *Heart and Minds*—screening notes. *Cinema Texas*, vol. 13, no. 3 (8 November 1977).

Haver, Ronald. *Casablanca*—program notes. Warner Brothers Pictures (printed in association with the American Film Institute), 1943.

Hawkins, Glenn. "The Starkly Real War." *Los Angeles Herald Examiner*, 24 September 1967.

Hearts and Minds—press packet. Paramount Pictures, 1975.

Herr, Michael. *Dispatches*. New York: Alfred A. Knopf, 1978.

"High Pressure Selznick Scripts Written while Cameras Grind." *New York Herald Tribune*, 16 June 1944.

Hill, Gladwin. "Grim Masquerade." *New York Times*, 16 October 1949.

Hopper, Hedda. "La Corbert Lured into Hit Role." *Los Angeles Times*, 29 October 1944.

Hyams, Jay. *War Movies*. New York: Gallery Books, 1984.

"It All Adds Up to 'Since You Went Away' ." *New York Times*, 25 May 1944.

Jordan, Richard. Press information for *Crimson Tide*. Hollywood Pictures, 1995.

Keneally, Thomas. "The Story of a Hero in Hell." *Los Angeles Times*, 12 December 1995.

King, Susan. "John Irvin Climbed Mountains to Do 'Hill'." *Los Angeles Herald Examiner*, 27 August 1987.

Kinney, Doris G. "Recaptured Glory." *Life*, February 1990.

Klein, Henry. "The 'M.A.S.H.' Mystique: How One Film Made Such a Difference in So Many Careers." *Entertainment World*, 22 May 1970.

Langman, Larry, and Ed Borg. *Encyclopedia of American War Films*. New York: Garland Publishing, 1989.

Lanning, Michael, L. *Vietnam at the Movies*. New York: Fawcett Columbine, 1994.

Leyda, Jay, and Zina Voynov. *Eisenstein at Work*. New York: Pantheon Books, 1982.

Lumenick, Lou. "Ran: Beauty and Power from a Japanese Master." *The Record*, 27 September 1985.

MacPherson, Virginia. "Mr. Meredith Sold on Pyle." *Hollywood Citizen News*, 12 December 1944.

Marshall, Herbert, ed. *The Battleship Potemkin*. New York: Avon Books, 1978.

MASH—press kit. Twentieth Century Fox, 1970.

McCullough, David, ed. *The American Heritage Picture History of World War II*. New York: Simon & Schuster, 1966.

McGilligan, Patrick. *Robert Altman: Jumping Off the Cliff*. New York: St. Martin's Press, 1989.

Miller, Russell. *Nothing Less Than Victory: The Oral History of D-Day*. New York: William Morrow, 1993.

Mitchell, George J. "Making of 'All Quiet on the Western Front.'" *American Cinematographer*, September 1985.

Mosby, Aline. "Sam Goldwyn Puzzled—MacKinlay Kantor's Charges Baffle Him." *Citizen News*, 27 June 1947.

Mrs. Miniver—publicity releases. MGM Studios, 1942.

Napoleon—program notes. American Film Institute, 7 June 1982.

Nichols, David, ed. *Ernie's War*. New York: Random House, 1986.

Nightingale, Benedict. "Henry V Returns as a Monarch for This Era." *New York Times*, 5 November 1989.

"Nightmare into Epic." *New York Magazine*, 18 December 1978.

"Not All Quiet for Remarque." *The Literary Digest*, 12 October 1929.

Othman, Frederick C. "Chaplin Seeks Berlin Premiere of 'Dictator'." *Herald*, 27 May 1940.

The Oxford Dictionary of Quotations. Oxford, England: Oxford University Press, 1979.

Parish, James R. *The Great Combat Pictures*. Metuchen, N.J.: Scarecrow Press, 1990.

Patton—press releases and program. Twentieth Century Fox, 1968.

Pearsal, Phyllis. *Women at War*. Hampshire, England: Ashgate Editions, 1990.

Piaza, Alex. "Program Notes." *Cinema Texas*, vol. 18, no. 3 (8 August 1980).

"Preparing for Paraplegics." *Life*, 12 June 1950.

Price, Keith. "Battleship Potemkin." *Cinema Texas*, vol. 8, no. 18 (11 February 1975).

Pryor, Thomas, M. "The Boy Wonder of 'The Search'." *New York Times*, 25 April 1948.

_____. "History of 'The Search'." *New York Times*, 14 March 1948.

_____. "Hollywood Canvas." *New York Times*, 15 June 1958.

Rau, Neil. "Roman Gladiator Wired for Death." *Los Angeles Examiner*, 26 April 1957.

_____. "War Is Hell—Even at Studio!" *Los Angeles Examiner*, 12 July 1958.

"The Real Thing." *Weekend Outlook*, 20 February 1983.

Reed, Rex. "George Is on His Best Behavior." *New York Times*, 29 March 1970.

Renoir, Jean. *My Life and My Films*. New York: Atheneum, 1974.

Robertson, Nan. "Crowds Hail Kurosawa at Two 'Ran' Showings." *New York Times*, 29 September 1995.

Ryan, Desmond. "The Glories of 'Glory'." *Philadelphia Inquirer*, 21 January 1990.

_____. "Veering Away from Olivier's Henry V." *Philadelphia Inquirer*, 10 December 1989.

Ryan, James. "Get Me (Glub Glub) Rewrite." *New York Times*, 7 May 1995.

Saltzman, Barbara. "The Big Parade Arrives at Orpheum." *Los Angeles Times*, 18 August 1979.

Sarris, Andrew. "The Birth of a Nation or White Power Back When." *Village Voice*, 17 July 1979.

Saunders, John M. "The Filming of an Epic." Paramount Pictures program, 1927.

Schickel, Richard. "The Knights in the Sky Return." *Life*, 22 October 1971.

Scott, John L. "Movie's Aim: Tell Patton's Saga the Way It Happened." *Los Angeles Times*, 12 January 1969.

Sharbutt, Jay. "The Grunt's War, Take 1." *Los Angeles Times*, 25 May 1986.

Simovic, Progos. "How Hitler Saw the Great Dictator." *Yugoslav Monthly Magazine*, October 1963.

Since You Went Away—program. *The Hollywood Reporter*, 4 August 1944.

Slide, Anthony. *All Quiet on the Western Front*—program. American Motion Picture Arts and Sciences screening, 27 September 1976.

Smith, Jack. "King Reflects on His Parade." *Los Angeles Times*, 19 March 1978.

Sorel, Edward. "La Grande Illusion." *Esquire*, June 1980.

Spartacus—production notes. Bryna Productions and Universal Pictures, 1960.

Stern, Seymour. "The Birth of a Nation"—special monograph supplement to *Sight and Sound*. Index series no. 3, summer 1945.

"Still Lively." *New Yorker*, 5 August 1950.

The Story of G.I. Joe—program notes. *Cinema Texas*, vol. 10, no. 3 (30 March 1976).

Strauss, Theodore. "Notes on the New Chaplin Film." *New York Times*, 18 August 1940.

Suid, Lawrence H. *Guts and Glory: Great American War Movies*. Reading, Mass.: Addison Wesley Publishing, 1978.

Tajiri, Larry. "Long Search for an Ending." *Denver Post*, 10 September 1964.

Terkel, Studs. *The Good War*. New York: Pantheon Books, 1984.

Tomme, Joy. *The Ritz Movie Guide—A New Olivier?* The Ritz Movie Theater, Philadelphia, 1989.

Toronto Film Society Program—Film-Buff Series A. 11 November 1984.

Turner, Richard. "The Worst Years of Our Lives." *New Times*, 20 March 1978.

Twelve O'Clock High—publicity release. Twentieth Century Fox, 2 August 1949.

Van Gelder, Robert. "Chaplin Draws a Keen Weapon." *New York Times Magazine*, 8 September 1940.

Wade, Nichola. "Henry V vs. Henry V: Branagh's Victory at Agincourt." *New York Times*, 6 February 1989.

Wallon, Norman S. *Eisenstein: A Documentary Portrait*. New York: E.P. Dutton, 1977.

Ward, Geoffrey. "A New Film, 'Glory,' Both Corrects and Distorts the Historical Record." *Vogue*, January 1990.

Warga, Wayne. "'M.A.S.H.' Mangles Filmmaking Axiom." *Los Angeles Times*, 8 March 1970.

_____. "Voight's Rising Star—Slow but Steady." *Los Angeles Times*, 19 February 1978.

Wellos, Robert. "Navy Casts a Wary Eye at Disney's 'Tide.'" *Los Angeles Times*, 28 June 1994.

"Wilde Denies He Piled on Sadism." *Variety*, 2 August 1967.

Wolf, William. "World War II Revisited in Spain for Patton." *Los Angeles Times*, 18 May 1969.

"'Wop' vs. 'Eternity': Real Maggio Sues over Frank Sinatra Character." *Hollywood Citizen News*, 26 March 1954.

Worcester, Marjorie. "Marjorie Worcester on Location." *Hollywood Reporter*, 19 July 1977.

Zinnemann, Fred. "On Using Non-Actors in Pictures." *New York Times*, 8 January 1950.

INDEX

PHOTO CREDITS